A Marathon of Purpose

A Journey through Life, Love & Legacy

By

Dr. Michael J. Marx,
Family & Friends

Copyright page

Dedication

This book is dedicated to all those individuals Michael reached out to throughout his life and touched in a formative and meaningful way. This is also dedicated to those whose lives Michael was yet to affect. He would have encouraged you to find your passion, work hard achieving it, and create a purposeful life for yourself and those who surround you. "Be the change you want to see in the world." Ghandi

Acknowledgement

Michael and I spent five months collecting his stories in the development of this book before he was too weak to continue. Thereafter, family members, and countless friends and colleagues from as close as North Carolina to as far as Australia and Indonesia have contributed earnest testimonies and anecdotes. Many thanks to all of you. Although all the contributions could not be included in the text, each helped us celebrate his life and helped us process our loss. Much appreciation goes to Michael's colleague, Debbie Fawcett, for her guidance and expertise throughout this process, and for being our emotional ballast.

Mostly, I acknowledge my sister-in-law, Joy Marx, who spent innumerable hours writing, editing, and collaborating with me on every detail in the face of her own suffering and grief. Joy and my brother formed a life together 42 years ago, and she never wavered in her devotion and support of Michael's goals. The life and love she provided was exemplary and formed the structure in which Michael was able to thrive.

Elizabeth H. Marx

Table of Contents

Joy

Wife, Soulmate, Belover

"This is my beloved; this is my friend."
Song of Solomon 5:16 (NIV)

Michael was my best friend and soulmate for 42 years. In private we would occasionally call each other "Belover," which comes from the above-mentioned Bible verse.

2 Timothy 4:7 "I have fought the good fight, I have finished the race, and I have remained faithful." Michael's life and legacy is best exemplified by this verse. We don't sprint towards the goal, but we work steadily and faithfully.

Michael left us exactly six months ago at the time of this writing. Spending so much time with his thoughts and words makes me feel (in a way) like he is still with us. His permanent departure from my life on this earth still doesn't seem real. I am comforted that Michael was so passionately looking forward to entering heaven where he could praise and glorify God forever.

I am delighted that we can share Michael's thoughts, desires and passions in this book as well as the tremendous impact he had on so many people.

Michael

I've had hundreds of phone conversations in which I've reached out to old friends to tell them I love them and to tell them how glad I am that they've been part of my life. No, this is not a random  activity. I'm doing this because I'm in an end-of-life scenario. As I write these words, I am surviving brain cancer but don't have long to live. By the time you read these words, I might be long gone. So, I'm on a mission to spread love. And one way I'm doing this is by asking everyone that I meet an intimate question. First, I tell them that I have just had brain surgery. They look at me with sympathy. It gives me a little bit of license to maybe cross the protocol line, "You have loved ones, don't you?" They look at me, and they say, "Yes, sir, I do." I respond, "So, I will tell you this. Don't wait until you're near the end of life to tell those people that you love them and you're so glad that they are part of your life." I have done this hundreds of times.

As a result, I hope that this book will help us focus on other people. In the end, the most important thing is not what we've done or accomplished, but the love relationships we've been able to maintain and grow. I hope that's why you're reading this book. Jesus is the reason why I'm writing it.

A memoir writer typically talks about him/herself all the time. One of my friends who recently finished her memoir called it a 'Me More' book. Alternately, this memoir is intended to serve you, the reader. Since my diagnosis, brain surgery, and end-of-life contemplations, I have become even more focused on others than I had already been. One of my friends commented, "Michael, your story inspires me. I want to be more 'other-focused' as you've become." Oh, that sounds good. I want my story to inspire people. My wish for you, dear reader, is that these words will inspire you to look beyond your own situation to see how you can help other people.

By sharing stories of significant events, I hope that it will give you the context for why spreading love is more important to me than my normal task-oriented life. I tend to concentrate on the next step, the next resource, the next line item on the checklist. In that regard, the apple doesn't fall far from the tree in the Marx family. Ask my sister who is helping to collect my stories and to prepare this memoir. I sincerely thank her for her time and effort.

A little about me: As an executive coach, I help people become leaders of their business entities, maximize the business' potential and elevate their outcomes.

I am also a life coach instructor - I train people in life coaching. I'm a Certified Master Christian Coach and a Master Certified Coach

(MCC) with the International Coaching Federation. I earned a doctorate in adult education with an emphasis on adult learning.

I have more credentials than I know what to do with. None of them make me an effective professional. I'm told that what makes me an effective professional is my ability to listen and think about the situation to help the client come up with their own solutions. Apparently, I do that very well because I have clients who depend on me to help them grow as individuals and with their  businesses. That's what I do, and at my core, that's who I am. It is my stated life goal to help people move forward with energy and purpose. It matters little to me whether that's in giant steps, or in baby steps. The important thing is that when I interact with people, they can move forward, and I can help them get there. That's who I am. Thank you for reading.

> *Amanda:* From our discussions after class to the work we did with Coaching Suicide Awareness, your love for God and others shined. Your zest and zeal for life kept me going when things were hard, and, for that, I will forever be grateful. You took the time to check in with me in a busy season of my life— which felt very much like you threw me a lifeline when I was drowning. You always helped me see a different perspective, another approach, or a better frame. Guess that's why you are such an amazing coach!

Vern: In the last months of Michael's life, we had many discussions on our journey together since 2012. At the end there were two priorities that Michael had.

The first was prayer. He had people he prayed for in 33 states as well as in other countries. He always mentioned that he prayed for my wife and me first since we were in the State of Maine. In his prayers he would start in the east, then move south and west.

The second focus was asking people, but especially men, "Did your father tell you he loved you?" He found that most men had never experienced such a deep and personal question. If not, he would say I love you and so does your heavenly Father." Michael would then talk about the Father.

This second focus was very moving to me. Over the time since Michael's death, I have tried to pass this along by asking men in my circle, "Did your father tell you he loved you?" If they answered "No," I would do exactly what Michael did by saying, "Well, I love you and the Father in heaven loves you too." There were men that had a very tough character that when the question was asked, they wept.

I plan to continue this legacy and ask others I meet to also do so. The benefits are many including leading to forgiveness and getting to know the Father.

Elizabeth

Sister, Ghostwriter

No words could express the shock of Michael's health crisis that unfurled in Europe (August 2023). From that point forward, our lives were in turmoil, and I felt as though I had been struck by an unexpected blow. I felt so helpless. How could I be there for

Michael, Elizabeth, Fred

Joy and Michael when they were dealing with this nightmare?

Michael had a lot of time and not much to occupy it when he returned from Slovakia following his brain surgery. How could he stay engaged with others and continue to fulfill his purpose? How could I help entertain him during this challenging time? In October, I came up with an idea to spend an hour each weekday with him on the phone and dubbed it "Michael and Me Time." No matter where I was or what I was in the middle of, I was at my desk at the right hour to capture his thoughts, stories, wit, and lessons. Michael enjoyed the challenge and outlined his narratives mentally before sharing them with me. It supported him cognitively and emotionally, and it revealed to me so many aspects of Michael and his life that I did not know. At one point, I shared with him that he had become more just than a sibling; he had become a valued friend.

I knew all along how short my time with Michael was becoming, so I considered every hour I spent with him a privilege and an honor. I do not regret the hours that went into this venture in the slightest; I only wish I had had more time to enjoy his humor and passions.

This curated compilation of Michael's musings was intended to be a gift from Michael to all of you who knew him and treasured him as a friend and colleague. It will give you a peek into his life from the formative years through his final months.

On April 30, 2024, Michael Marx took his last breath at the early age of 62 and left us to sit at the feet of his heavenly Father. Michael's entire life was centered on spiritual outreach to family, friends, and strangers.

When Michael died, his eyes were closed, but his heart was open.

A Mother's Love Letter

Joy: Michael's mother Edith wrote the following letter in November 2015. It was the last she wrote to him before she passed away in 2016. This letter is a treasure and gives a perspective on Michael's origins.

Michael - named after the highest angel in heaven, "the Archangel!" Michael was and is a gift from God, chosen to be one of His representatives on earth. From the minute he opened his eyes, he was declared to be a miracle!! Michael's conception was ordained by the Lord... Let me recall the circumstances.

Arlene Pearson, our neighbor, bought a new organ. It had three levels of keyboards, the most elaborate house organ on the market. She invited about 50 people to celebrate her joy. Food and wine were in abundance. Until the morning hours, Arlene played sacred hymns, folk songs, dance music, etc. We came home tired and happy. You were conceived. Such JOY! (I wanted 12 children.) Dr. Vanderbeck, a practicing catholic with 10 children of his own, confirmed the BLESSING. Because of RH negative blood, I was not a candidate for motherhood. Anthony, who died in 1958, had the results of the RH factor. What was the answer for your survival? Both Dr. Vanderbeck and I agreed – Prayer!

At that time, I was a kindergarten teacher in Fairlawn. The owner of the school and I were bosom friends. It was hard to give up my job, but I did. My future was devoted to prayer. I informed the convent in Vienna to join me, and they did. Every morning Dr. Vanderbeck and I attended Mass–with communion–at Mount Carmel church in Ridgewood. Three to four times per week my blood was tested, and a hormone shot was given–after we joined in prayer–in faith believing that we <u>would</u> be granted our request.

The delivery took many hours. When I finally could take in information, I was told that the child and mother were at the brink of death. Two doctors attended the birth. Both declared that us being alive was the greatest miracle in their practice! Both Dr. Vanderbeck and I attribute the results to months of prayer.

At the age of six you broke through the ice on the lake. David Toth, much younger than you, ran to get his mother. She crawled on her hands and knees to get to you. You wore a heavy outfit, soaked with water. She could not lift you... she prayed! We took you to the Emergency Room. A team of nurses, doctors, etc. worked on you for six hours. The prognosis was not good. Finally, you were sent home to die. It was Thursday evening, my bible study time with Esther. That evening they did not have bible study. They spent TWO hours in prayer for you. The next morning you showed some signs of recovery.

Very early in your life you developed rheumatoid arthritis in your knees. They were swollen and extremely painful. You could not walk comfortably or run. Because there was no cure, you were on heavy painkillers. Before you started seventh grade, you decided to be a football player. The doctor said, "out of question." At that time, I was also with a prayer group on a weekly basis, in another city. We learned and prayed for divine healing, deliverance, etc. The group, which also included men with authority, prayed for you. The swelling went down, pain stopped, etc. When you entered seventh grade, I requested football, and you were examined for it by two doctors. On the papers I filled out, I stated: rheumatic fever and the medication taken in the past. They both agreed that you never had it, nor ever had taken the medicine which had grave aftereffects.

As you know, your father and I attended every game, home and elsewhere. He and Joe Richardson were your cheerleaders. I was sitting while they were screaming. Early on I realized that in football, injuries are possible—mainly concussions. So, I sat crocheting and praying for both teams. Not one of you were injured in all those years...

I am going to go back to your entry to kindergarten. Shortly after you started, the teacher requested to see me. When I arrived, I found the teacher upset. She told me that she had to put you in the corner. That did not work, so she sat you on a chair in the hall. That did not work. The problem: she had five children from Lakeview Drive in her room. You and four more, the other four did not follow any of her requirements unless they had your approval. With other words, you were their leader, and they would not take directions from anyone else.

You continued to be a leader all through life. The Lord's wisdom and His guidance are a very predominant factor in your life... I thank God for choosing Joy to be your partner to serve Him and mankind. The Lord and I rejoice in your life, and He is glad that He created you. Your life and future are in His hands, and He has many good plans and blessings for your life.

Give thanks for unknown blessings already on the way. Personally, I thank the Lord for the honor of choosing me to be your mom. I have always loved you in the past, love you today, and will love you all the future days ahead.

These are just a couple of the verses the Lord has given me for you:

"Trust in the Lord with all your heart; do not depend on your own understanding. Seek his will in all you do, and He will show you which path to take." Proverbs 3:5-6

"I pray that God, the source of hope, will fill you completely with joy and peace because you trust in him. Then you will overflow with confident hope through the power of the Holy Spirit." Romans 15:13.

With loving prayers and HUGS,

Mom

Childhood in New Jersey

Grandma, you stink!

"Grandma, you stink," I blurted out, much to my parents' consternation. I was just a child, no more than five, but the memory lingers as if it happened yesterday. Grandma had come from Hungary to help when I was born in 1961 and to spend time with her youngest son. She found work in a Jewish deli and  would come home every evening carrying the scent of onions and gefilte fish—a cloud that followed her, distinct and persistent. For a child, it was too strong to ignore.

Grandma's smell became a symbol of her presence, a constant reminder of her dedication and hard work. She was adamant that we would finish everything on our plates, a habit ingrained in me to this day. At the time, it was just an inconvenience, but as I look back now, I realize it was her way of ensuring we were taken care of, of showing her love. This insistence on finishing what was in front of us went beyond food—it was a lesson in commitment and perseverance.

In her worn depression-era dresses and single cardigan, Grandma was a paradox. While the adults around us spoke German, often leaving us children in the dark, her presence was both comforting and overbearing. She criticized American life as "too fast, too loose," longing for the simplicity of her homeland. Her disapproval of even the smallest things, like having more than one sweater or coat, made her seem out of touch with our American way of life. Yet, it was her old-world values that planted the seeds of discipline and work ethic in me.

Reflections on Hard Work

Through her, I learned that hard work was not just about toiling for the sake of it but was a form of service. The Protestant work ethic that she embodied wasn't simply about labor; it was a call to serve, to contribute meaningfully. As I grew up, this belief evolved into my understanding that work was a path to serve God. Grandma's influence became a cornerstone of my spiritual journey — work as a calling, not an obligation. Her scent may have been off-putting to my young senses, but it was the smell of sacrifice, of a life dedicated to others.

Family Dynamics & Cultural Clash

The dynamic between Grandma and my parents was strained. She never quite approved of my mother, who she felt epitomized the decadence of American culture; ironic since she was also from war-torn Europe. My mother, despite her best efforts, could never seem to impress Grandma. They were two women from vastly different worlds—my mother, a product of the 1960s, who embraced convenience foods like TV dinners and instant coffee, and Grandma, with her traditional Hungarian dishes. My mother's willingness to adapt and learn, becoming a sophisticated cook to match Grandma's standards, spoke volumes about her desire to bridge the gap. It was a subtle lesson in the complexity of family relationships and the often-silent sacrifices we make for each other.

Father's Role & The Knickerbockers

My father, though present, was a man of few words, especially when it came to showing affection. His relationship with Grandma was more formal than familial. He busied himself with work and played in a German Oktoberfest-style band, The Knickerbockers. Music was his escape, his solace, and perhaps his way of preserving a connection to his heritage. On weekends, he would load up our '62 Rambler with instruments, sheet music, and us kids in tow, journeying across upstate New York to bars and parks. Those outings were less about family bonding and more about fulfilling a duty, yet they left an indelible mark on me.

The music and the trips were my early exposure to the idea of passion intertwined with discipline. My father's commitment to his band, even amidst a strained relationship with his mother, taught me that one could pursue their passion while shouldering family responsibilities. He demonstrated that life's duties and one's passions could coexist, even if imperfectly. This became a foundational lesson as I navigated my own calling later in life.

Mother's Influence & Cultural Assimilation

My mother, on the other hand, was a figure of quiet strength. Torn between her calling to become a nun and her desire to have a family, she found a way to incorporate both into her life. She was, in many ways, a nun at heart—a woman of deep faith, devotion, and discipline. She attended Mass every morning, a routine that was more than religious—it was her grounding ritual in a world that often felt too chaotic.

Despite Grandma's disapproval, my mother embraced the American lifestyle. She learned to cook and bake not just out of necessity but out of a desire to bridge cultural divides. Her adoption of Jewish deli foods and Yiddish culture was her way of honoring Grandma's world while maintaining her identity. My mother's efforts at assimilation and her subtle rebellion against Grandma's strict expectations taught me the importance of finding one's path amidst conflicting cultural narratives. She showed me that it's possible to honor the past while forging one's future.

Lakeview Drive: The Playground of Lessons

Lakeview Drive was not just our address; it was a microcosm of life's lessons. The diversity of cultures—the Dutch, the Catholics, the immigrants—created a vibrant tapestry of perspectives. It was here that I learned to navigate differences and found that despite cultural distinctions, there was a common thread of humanity that connected us all.

The brook that paralleled our street was a constant source of wonder and danger. Winters transformed the pond into an ice rink, a stage on which I learned both the thrill of adventure and the sting of failure. Skating taught me resilience—the willingness to fall and get back up again. Building treehouses with scrap wood from the local lumberyard was more than just play. It was my first experience in creating something from nothing, of using imagination and ingenuity to bring ideas to life.

As my friends and I moved from tree to tree, constructing precarious platforms, I learned the value of the process over product. Our final treehouse, built in the attic of our garage and wallpapered with posters, was a masterpiece by our standards. But in its completion, we found a void—we had been more fulfilled by the act of building than by the result itself. This realization was an early lesson in understanding that the journey, not the destination, often holds the most value. This lesson stayed with me, shaping my approach to life and the pursuit of meaning in my work.

Spiritual Foundation & Early Faith

Across from our house lived Barbara, who ran a weekly "kids' club"—her Dutch-reformed version of Sunday school. It was there, with flannel figures of Jesus, Mary, Paul, and Silas animated on a board, that the foundations of my spiritual understanding were laid. Those stories became more than mere tales; they were seeds planted in my young mind, growing into a faith that would become central to my life. The simplicity of those gatherings, the childlike wonder they inspired, laid the groundwork for a spiritual journey that has been evolving ever since.

The "kids' club" was a counterpoint to my Catholic upbringing, introducing me to the idea that spirituality transcends denominational boundaries. It taught me that faith was not confined to ritual but was a living, breathing aspect of daily life. The seeds of this early faith grew into a belief system that later informed my view of work as a calling—a way to serve God not just through ministry but in every endeavor.

Sharing the Gift of Compassion

The incident with the family across the street who lost their home to a fire was a turning point in my early development. As the youngest child, I was used to having things my way. Suddenly, my space, my toys, and even my family's attention had to be shared with six displaced children. It was a struggle. At the time, it felt like an intrusion, an unfair demand on my young self. But this experience planted the seeds of empathy and compassion in me.

Looking back, it was one of my first encounters with the idea of selflessness—putting others' needs above my own. Even though my initial reaction was resentment, the act of sharing became an unspoken lesson in what it means to be part of a community. Decades later, as I am dealing with my own illness, the compassion extended to me by others, including cards from those very same "kids," reminded me that the seeds of kindness planted in childhood can bear fruit when we need it the most.

Ridge Elementary: The Birthplace of Curiosity

Attending Ridge Elementary School was an education not just in academics but in the social fabric of society. The school was in an affluent town, but our street was the exception. Walking the mile and a half to school daily, often stopping to collect trinkets from a junk-laden property, taught me to see value in the discarded. My fascination with these found objects was more than a child's play; it was an early expression of creativity and resourcefulness, my tendency to repurpose what others overlooked.

My fourth-grade teacher was pivotal in shaping my intellectual curiosity. Her stories of world travels and her ability to intertwine music and poetry revealed a world far beyond Ridgewood. She taught us to listen to music not just as entertainment but as poetry, as a medium that conveyed deeper truths about human experience. This exposure to different forms of art and expression fostered in me a lifelong love of knowledge and an appreciation for the diverse ways people communicate their stories.

These early years, filled with seemingly ordinary events and interactions, laid the groundwork for the person I would become. From Grandma's stern yet loving insistence on finishing what was on my plate to the joy of building treehouses and the complex dynamics within my family, each moment contributed to the tapestry of my life. They were not just memories; they were lessons in love, work, faith, and the importance of finding joy in the journey itself.

These formative experiences have shaped my approach to life, work, and relationships. They instilled in me the belief that each moment, no matter how mundane, carries the potential to teach us about who we are and what we are meant to do. As I continue to serve others through my work and reflect on my spiritual journey, I see how these childhood moments, rich with love and learning, have influenced the legacy I hope to leave behind.

Debbie: Michael really enjoyed different kinds of music, and he enjoyed sharing music with others. During COVID, the song "The Blessing" (by Kari Jobe, Cody Carnes and Elevation Worship) was all over the internet. Michael's favorite version was with singers and people doing sign language. He told me that he "always wanted to learn sign language." During a visit years later, when he was dealing with cancer, I brought along my sign language book. For several hours we practiced different signs. "What's the sign for Lord? What's the sign for heaven? What's the sign for _____?" He was like a kid having so much fun learning. Thank you, Michael, for teaching me to always be learning with abandon, always be curious, share music whenever you have the opportunity, and give blessings over people you meet.

Claire: Michael is a dear friend who gave much of himself to keeping people whole and healthy. Wise, knowledgeable, deep, kind, gentle, ethical are all words that apply to this great soul.

Teen in North Carolina

In 1973, my father's employer moved his office from upstate New York to Greensboro, North Carolina, uprooting our family and taking us to a place that seemed like another world. I had grown up surrounded by the bustling energy of Ridgewood, New Jersey, just on the outskirts of New York City. In Greensboro, it was as if we'd landed in an entirely different culture. I remember the shock when we first arrived to find the town paralyzed by six inches of snow. Back in New Jersey, such a snowfall was a minor inconvenience, but here, it seemed to bring life to a halt. The realization that our new home didn't understand snow was just the beginning of my cultural adjustment.

Adapting to the North Carolinian Vernacular

The people of North Carolina were different, not just in their way of life but in their language. The first time I heard a North Carolinian speak, I was struck by the poetic cadence in their words. It was like listening to a hillbilly poet recite verses from an unwritten ballad. Their idiomatic expressions were an art form. One phrase that stood out to me was, "She's as cute as a speckled pup sitting under a red wagon," which I first heard on a radio advertisement. At the time, these expressions were confusing and felt like another language entirely. I was used to the straightforward "Yankee" talk of the North, but here, conversations were woven with metaphor and simile, turning the mundane into something almost lyrical.

In retrospect, this vernacular was more than just a way of speaking; it reflected their worldview. The people of North Carolina had a way of seeing life that turned the ordinary into something special. They were warm, loving, and deeply family-oriented, embodying a slower, more deliberate way of living that contrasted sharply with the hurried pace of the North. Their language was a doorway into this culture, teaching me to appreciate the subtleties and nuances of everyday experiences.

Cultural Differences & Dietary Curiosities

Food became another symbol of the cultural divide. North Carolinians had their own culinary traditions, some of which seemed peculiar to my Northern sensibilities. Take, for example, their approach to biscuits and gravy. Today, December 14, (2023) is National Biscuits and Gravy Day, and in honor of my years in North Carolina, Joy and I went to a local restaurant to indulge in this Southern delicacy. But the way North Carolinians consumed it was an art form. They crumpled biscuits into a tall glass, poured buttermilk over them, and ate the concoction with a long-handled spoon. It was a ritual I had never seen before or since. To my young mind, it was strange, yet it became a part of the North Carolinian charm that I grew to appreciate.

These culinary experiences, along with others, began to shape my understanding of culture. I realized that food was not just sustenance; it reflected the people and their values. The comfort and warmth embodied in a meal of biscuits and gravy mirrored the hospitality and warmth of the people. It was in these simple, everyday practices that I found the essence of what it meant to be a North Carolinian.

Guilford Middle School: A Cultural Shock

When I showed up for my first day at Guilford Middle School, I felt like I had entered the Twilight Zone. The language barrier was immediately apparent. In New Jersey, "Yes" was a simple affirmation, but here, it required the formality of "Yes, ma'am" or "Yes, sir." On that first day, the teacher directed me to sit at the fourth desk. "Yes," I replied, only to be scolded with a stern correction. I was stunned, not understanding what I had done wrong until a kind classmate whispered the appropriate response. This was my first lesson in Southern etiquette, and it wouldn't be my last.

Navigating the school cafeteria was another adventure. Grits and other Southern delicacies appeared on my tray, and I found myself wondering, once again, where I had landed. This was more than a geographical move; it was a shift in cultural paradigms. In class, we studied the Civil War and learned about the cotton gin, invented by Eli Whitney. At home, inspired by these lessons, I used cardboard, pressboard, and toothpicks to build a replica model of a cotton gin. I don't recall if this was a school project or simply a personal endeavor, but it marked the beginning of my habit of turning learning into creative expression. It was in these moments of adaptation and creativity that I started to carve out my place in this new world.

Finding My Identity Amidst Six Michaels

Sixth grade presented a new challenge: there were six boys named Michael in my class. In this sea of namesakes, I needed to distinguish myself. I took on extra projects and sought out ways to contribute to the classroom environment. If there was something lacking or a problem that needed solving, I volunteered to fix it. This desire to stand out and be useful was the beginning of my journey into finding my unique identity and purpose. I learned that I could use my skills to help others, a lesson that would become a defining aspect of my life.

Western Guilford High: A Crucible of Growth

Contrary to many people's experiences, I thoroughly enjoyed my high school years. Western Guilford High School offered a world of opportunities, and I dove in headfirst. The ninth grade drafting class was a revelation. For the first time, I could see a clear path for my future. I was hooked on the idea of preparing technical drawings and set my sights on becoming an architect. My high school years were filled with drawing and building models of houses, each project reinforcing my ambition to attend the architectural school at NC State University. My peers playfully called me "Archie Architect," but I wore the nickname with pride. It was a badge of honor that symbolized my dedication and passion.

High school also exposed me to the broader world of industrial arts. I learned the basics of metallurgy, welding, soldering, and woodworking. One of my proudest creations was a salad bowl carved from black mahogany. We still have that bowl to this day. I was advised to rub salad oil on it each time it held a salad to ensure its longevity. Made in 1977, the bowl remains in good condition — a testament to the lessons of care, craftsmanship, and the enduring value of things created with one's own hands.

The Rite of Passage: Driving, Dating & Work

Driving and dating were rites of passage that came with their own set of challenges. I soon realized that these new freedoms were expensive, prompting me to seek out jobs. My first job was at an architectural firm as an office boy. I printed blueprints and prepared paperwork for on-site work. This job was more than a means to an end; it was an opportunity to immerse myself in the world of architecture. It was here that I developed a taste for black coffee, the only free beverage available. It became an acquired taste that has stuck with me ever since.

My other jobs were varied. I worked as a handyman and mowed lawns, including for Alice, a friend of my mother's. I took care of her house for a month, dusting her collection of antiques and knickknacks. At the end of the summer, Alice gave me her father's car—a 1969 Plymouth Fury III. It was a gas-guzzler, getting maybe eight miles to the gallon, but I didn't care. At 16, having my own car was a milestone. It symbolized independence and a newfound sense of responsibility.

With a car, a girlfriend, and some money in my pocket, my best friend Rick Smith and I spent our time exploring the freedom that came with our teenage years. We drove around, attended church events, and developed a routine of visiting Pizza Hut every Sunday night. We would tell jokes and even compete to see who had the best "bad dad" joke. My penchant for these jokes led me to become the unofficial high school weatherman. Every morning, I would listen to the news, jot down the weather report, and deliver it to my classmates. It was a small role, but it gave me a sense of purpose and belonging.

Reflecting on Growth & Adaptation

Looking back, my teenage years in North Carolina were a period of profound growth and adaptation. From the initial cultural shock to finding my identity among six other Michaels, every experience taught me something valuable. I learned to appreciate the nuances of a culture vastly different from my own. I discovered the importance of using my skills to contribute to a community, a lesson that has guided my career and life choices ever since.

The time spent in Greensboro was not just about transitioning from childhood to adulthood; it was about learning to adapt, finding joy in the simple things, and understanding that growth often comes from stepping outside of one's comfort zone. The Southern culture, with its unique vernacular, dietary quirks, and social etiquette, expanded my worldview and taught me to find beauty in diversity. My experiences at Western Guilford High School solidified my passion for architecture and instilled in me a sense of purpose. These years were not just a chapter in my life; they were a crucible that shaped my values, ambitions, and the path I would follow into adulthood.

Rick Smith, Michael's best friend (May 2024):

Did you know Michael had something in common with my hair? They both left me way too soon!

I realized when someone asked, what was he like? You can't explain Michael Joseph Marx in just a word or two. In fact, he was so unique each person would have something different to say about him. Well, here is my version in its simplest form.

If someone asked me to sweep the floor I would do it but the whole time I would be worried, am I doing a good enough job? On the other hand, if someone asked Michael to sweep the floor, he would gladly do it. When he was finished you would have some modifications to your broom, or maybe even a new broom that he made from whatever he could find. You would also receive 3 to 5 suggestions on how to keep the floor from getting so dirty.

When the two of us would go out to eat, it was always an adventure. At some point Michael would say something like "did you notice the waiter keeps using the phrase 'xyz'? We need to check with him and see how we can help him. Or I couldn't help but overhear the couple at the next table. I think we need to pray with them or at least pray for them. Me: Nope. All I noticed was I was hungry, and the food was good. But Michael would want to call the waiter over to see what was going on with him so we could pray.

When the two of us would hang out and swap stories and talk of times gone by, Michael would listen to every word intently, but when you stopped speaking, he would get that little grin on his face and say, "uh huh." Now that uh-huh was the clue you were about to be corrected, or one of his memories/stories was about to be shared, or possibly just a cheesy one-liner joke was coming.

Now when it comes to his stories, I could not compare to him. Michael had been to places and done things I could only imagine, but when it came to the one-liner corny jokes, I was the better one. I always knew when I got in a good one-liner that Michael liked. My line was going to live on, and many more people would hear it because it now belonged to Michael!

Again, Michael was such a unique person in the way he approached life and certainly in the way he faced death.

From these three examples I have given, there are many things that can be learned but at the core of these examples are three basic truths:

1. Always leave a situation better than you found it.

2. Strive to see more than just the person on the surface.

3. Uplift everyone you meet either with a kind correction, a feeling you can relate to, and let them know that they matter, or at the very least make them smile with a cheesy one-liner.

Thank you, Michael, for all you gave us!

Rick Smith

My First Ski Adventure

Since my brother Fred was big on skiing, I wanted to find out what all the fuss was about. The church youth group provided the first chance to learn a sport, which would be very influential in my life.

We went to the Appalachian ski area near Asheville. Technologically, it was one of the worst ski experiences I've ever had. The rented ski boots were ancient and uncomfortable. No one was available to help us correctly fit into them. Eventually, the whole group of teenagers was geared up and moved onto the snow. There was no actual instruction nor program for new skiers.

An instructor came over to the group of us and taught us to point the front of our skis together into a snowplow position, which is the worst thing you can teach new skiers. Use the snowplow; don't go too fast; glide to the next lift. Wow, I thought, this is more fun than water skiing!

I remember my friend Brad did not slow down, and he went full speed all the way down to the bottom and ran into a snowplow. Sliding and gliding, up and down, falling and getting frustrated. I felt pleased with my first ski experience and quickly decided that this would be one of my favorite sports. Since then, I have skied all over Europe and North America and am a certified ski instructor.

Football

I tried out for the junior varsity football team and made it because I was fast. I was the second fastest guy on the football team behind the halfback. I was so fast, the coach wanted me to be a wide receiver, but I couldn't catch the ball. So, they made me a defensive end instead.

I played football to stay in shape for the track team, which is what I really wanted to do. I ran the 100-yard dash and the 200-yard dash and the 440-yard dash, all on a relay team. I loved the precision handoff of the aluminum baton between four people running sprints, with only microseconds for the handoff. I was never a stellar athlete since my eye-hand coordination was lousy. My hand coordination didn't catch up with my body until I was 35 years old, which was a relief because by that time I had a son, and I wanted to teach him how to throw and catch. To my surprise, when I had the opportunity at 35 to teach my son Milton to throw and catch, I could finally execute a catch myself for the first time in my life.

> *Fred:* Without regard to Michael's skills of self-assessment, he WAS built like a football player. I, on the other hand, am built like a scarecrow. The above-mentioned story took place during a rare family gathering in North Carolina. In between doing nothing followed by doing nothing else, Michael, young Milton, my young son Jeremy and I, decided to play a little football in our parents' backyard. On the very first play from scrimmage, the ball was snapped and I was tackled by Michael, the Mack truck. Broken collarbone. End of game. Good times.

One day, one of our church leaders was talking to the head coach about the boys from church and asking how they were doing on the football team. The coach said about me, "If I had 22 players that had the heart and determination of Michael Marx, we would win the state championship every year. People should imitate Michael Marx because he's got the heart and soul of a winning team player." This is probably one of the most meaningful compliments I've ever received in my lifetime.

One of the things that attracts people to me is knowing that when they get into my circle of influence, it's going to be with power, devotion, commitment, and determination. At a team meeting a couple of weeks ago, one of my team members said, "Listening to Michael Marx for an hour when he's excited about something is inspiring." I would encourage everyone reading these words to encourage the teenagers they know to get plugged into the right crowd. It makes a life-long difference.

Goodie Two Shoes?

My sister remembers me affectionately as having a goody two shoes persona because I "never did anything wrong."

Believe it or not, there are a lot of kids who grow up never doing anything seriously wrong, and I was one of them. I hung out with friends who were good kids, too. We never got into fights. We were never suspended from school. I earned good grades for the most part. If you had mentioned me to any passing adults who knew me, they would say, "Michael Marx, he's a good kid."

But not 100% of the time. Let me tell you about some of those off moments since I don't think it is appropriate to only tell you about the exemplary things. I think most American teenagers experience things they would rather have blotted off their record.

It's hard for an American teenager to avoid alcohol. I only got drunk once. My best friend Rick and I decided that we had no idea what it felt like to be drunk. So, we asked a 19-year-old friend to help us with the experience. One Friday night we had vodka, a nice bottle of fresh squeezed orange juice and a pack of cigarettes for a full experience. The cigarettes were terrible. I still don't like cigarettes or tobacco, or anything smoked.

Teenagers are exposed to alcohol at parties. Everyone is drinking. Teens think it's cool. If everyone's having a beer, no 17-year-old is going to refuse. You would become very unpopular with your peers very quickly.

Early in my university freshman year, on a Friday afternoon, we would go out in front of the dorms and throw a frisbee and drink beer. In college I learned very quickly that there are three types of beer. There's good beer, there's better beer, and there's free beer. I learned all about good beer while in Germany, but in my freshman year in college, it only had to be free to be good.

There's also a difference between cheap wine and very, very expensive wine, none of which I've ever been able to distinguish which is ironic because our cousins run the Bozóky vineyard and produce fine Hungarian wines. In fact, my cousin Monica once asked me to consider becoming their German distributor for the family winery, specifically for the Mori Riesling wines. I was honored that she would ask. However, with a deviated septum, I can't smell my way out of a paper bag. I literally can't distinguish between a good or sour glass of wine. I would have liked to sell

Bozóky wine; instead, I settled for picking up two bottles when I visited Hungary in August 2023, the week I discovered I had brain cancer. I was determined to make it back to the United States with the wine so I could share it with the family on Thanksgiving. This served as a major motivation for me to make it back from Europe.

Thanksgiving 2023: Michael, Joy, Kat, Milton

Back to the overall topic: good kids and bad kids. I'm of the opinion that somewhere between the ages 17 and 27, kids (young adults) are going to start experimenting. It could be more dangerous if they had never experimented. In my opinion, a responsible parent should encourage their responsible children to be responsible while being irresponsible. In other words, don't do something stupid just to prove that you can be just as naughty as anyone else and survive. If you're going to be irresponsible, then be responsible while being irresponsible. Learn to do it in a safe way. Encourage responsible children to take chances, to take risks that get their adrenaline flowing. Let them experience the ability to walk that tightrope. Participate in a ropes course; drive a go-cart. Encourage kids to have fun, even a little bit on the wild side, just to the extent that it is helping them expand their horizons and broaden their sense of self-worth.

Denominations

My family was Roman Catholic until I was around six years old. I still cherish how the Catholic Church creates sacred moments. You just don't stop and pray. You create a sacred place. And then when everybody is calm and focused, you pray. I did not originally appreciate liturgy, but now I love it. Every word of the prayers, the covenants and the blessings have been thought out for hundreds of years, which make them very rich in meaning. I've evolved from Catholic to Baptist to charismatic, back to liturgical, and currently I'm in a Baptist church again.

None of us must do anything to earn the favor of God. What God wants us to do is worship Him in what we do. In other words, what we do becomes our act of worship. This is a concept, which I never really understood until my mid-30s. All the work that I was doing in the church and for the church, was an act of worship. When I was a teenager, I didn't realize that I was actively worshiping God with my talents. Being a leader and being where He needed me to be at the time was indeed a form of worship.

Guilford Baptist Church

My father became the Minister of Music at Guilford Baptist Church, consequently the youth group at the church became my clique. Larry Wakefield, the youth pastor who later became a missionary in Mexico, was not only my mentor but also played a significant role in my spiritual development as a teenager. His commitment to leave his home for the sake of spreading the gospel in another country impacted me greatly. Additionally, Larry was getting his master's degree in theater. Larry taught church drama and a little bit of pantomime to a few of us in the youth group, which also became extremely influential in my life. Due to the skills Larry taught me, I even performed in a couple of high school plays and musicals.

I became the leader of the church's youth council, which would meet every week to plan activities. We would receive approval for various events such as going bowling or going on hayrides. I was literally running the youth department of Guilford Baptist Church. I was learning that leadership is a key to success in life.

When Larry and his family moved to Mexico as missionaries, another youth pastor arrived who was not a good person. This man made a significant (negative) impact on my life when he sat me down one day and said, "I want you to stop." "Stop what?" I asked. He said, "Stop what you're doing. You're doing my job and you're threatening my livelihood." I was just 17 years old, so I didn't understand the allegation. Nevertheless, I felt very threatened. Church had been a safe place for me to learn and grow, and to be with my friends. I could experiment with leadership and follow what I thought God wanted me to do. This man really knocked me off my pedestal. It left me disillusioned with the church for several years. Ultimately, that youth pastor was fired, but the damage had been done.

Education

I graduated from high school with honors. My success in high school was attributable in part to my involvement in church. Activities kept me out of trouble. Bad things can happen in any high school. Due to my position as a youth leader in the church, I never wanted to tarnish that reputation and consequently stayed out of trouble through high school. I credit the Baptist Church for helping me do that.

I applied for architectural school at North Carolina State and was accepted. At that time, it was the number five architectural school in the country.

Young Adult in Oklahoma

Since I had just completed my first year as an architectural student at North Carolina State University in 1981, I applied for a job working in construction. The interview went something like this.

The contractor observed, "You're an architectural student; you can read blueprints." I agreed. He said, "What is that right there?" pointing at an object. I said, "It's the foundation for a steel column." He agreed, then asked, "Can you dig the hole that we need to pour the concrete in?" I said I could and that I'd come back the next day to dig the hole. He said, "Oh, no need for tomorrow. I need it right now."

Despite being in interview clothes versus work clothes, I grabbed a shovel, went outside, and dug the hole according to specifications. The contractor looked at me and said, "You can come back tomorrow." Before I knew it, I was promoted to the role of hole digger foreman. Shortly after, I became the crew chief for a construction project at Friend's Home West. Despite most of the crew having 15 years of construction experience, I was the only one who could read blueprints. It felt great to lead people in their 30s at the age of 19. Our main task was to dig around 27 holes for anchoring the steel columns.

While working, I couldn't shake the persistent thought of attending Oral Roberts University, even though they didn't offer an architectural program. This thought continued to nag at me and was beginning to drive me crazy.

Sometime around the first week of August, I said to God, "Okay, that's it. I'm going to drive 20 hours to Tulsa." I decided to just show up without a plan or an idea of what was going to happen. I had to get this "message" out of the back of my head!

Upon arriving in Tulsa, the campus of Oral Roberts University (ORU) unfurled before me like some sort of Christian Disneyland, a collection of magical buildings. Since I had no idea what to do nor where to go, I started with the admission's office.

I was in a rebellious state at that point. The negative experience with my youth pastor had really set me back a couple of notches. I had spent that summer partying, spreading my wings, and finding out what it meant to live on the wild side.

I was directed to Jim's office and sat down. Jim asked, "How may I help you?" I said in a matter-of-fact voice, "Well, the Lord keeps telling me to go to ORU. Now I'm here. I want you to tell me why." I explained my background and then my rebellion. He listened to me and then said, "Okay, this is what I want you to do. Go down to the microbiology department." I argued, "Microbiology! Were you not listening? I'm an architectural student." He responded, "I want you to see Dr. Vernon Scoles, who oversees microbiology at ORU. He is researching a link between unforgiveness and cancer." It was a high-profile department. Off I went to Dr. Scoles' office.

Dr. Scoles urged me to share my story, which I did. I was surprised when Dr. Scoles said, "I want you to work as one of my assistants because I want to keep an eye on you." Subsequently, I was employed as an assistant to handle photocopying and filing for the microbiology department. I appreciated having the job.

I hadn't even applied as a student; the semester had already commenced. I had arrived at an already overcrowded university; there was no "room in the inn." There were no accommodations for unexpected students.

Efforts were made to reach out to people and requests were put forth. Ultimately, two jazz musicians, Jeff and Steve, offered to share their room with me. Despite the rooms being designed for only two individuals, a third auxiliary bed was obtained from storage. Three young men in a tiny room; it was fantastic. I gained extensive knowledge about jazz music from Jeff and Steve during that semester.

It was also a semester of significant spiritual growth! As I felt drawn towards missions, I joined a street outreach ministry as an extracurricular activity. One of the mandatory classes at ORU was oral communication. I barely managed to get into it. By chance, Joy Miller also ended up in the same class. Since we were both part of a presentation team, we scheduled a team meeting one evening. I arrived late due to my involvement in street ministry in downtown Tulsa. I apologized to the group, explaining my whereabouts. Joy thought, "Oh, this is a pretty cool guy. He's spending his evenings doing street ministry on the dark side of

Tulsa." That's how we met. After working on the project together, Joy and I became friends.

I also applied for a summer mission team. Due to my background in architecture, I was initially assigned to the team going to Brazil, where we were supposed to use local materials like jungle wood to construct huts for jungle churches. As an architecture student, the project appealed to my enduring architectural aspirations. Surprisingly, I never went to Brazil. The team in Switzerland was planning to engage in street evangelism with pantomime in collaboration with a local youth group. Given my experience in drama, I had some knowledge of mime. The director suggested that I consider switching from the Brazil team to the Switzerland team. I inquired if they spoke German or French, and the director responded, "I think they speak German." I remarked, "There's just one issue with that because I don't speak German." In reply, he stated, "First and foremost, we need you for your mime skills, not for your German." "Okay," I said. "I understand the mime aspect. So, I don't have to speak, right?" "Correct. I noticed in your records that you're taking German, albeit failing German." This was accurate. German was the only academic course I ever failed. I spent four to six hours a day trying to learn German; it was challenging from the very beginning and never eased up. I would go to the library and sit down with Joy so she could go over my class notes with me. With her assistance and six hours a day, I eventually secured a passing grade in German.

That summer (1982), I traveled to Switzerland with Joy and two other teammates from ORU. After spending a month in Switzerland, we journeyed to Bilbao, Spain, with the Swiss Youth with a Mission (YWAM) evangelism team, which was performing street drama during the Mundial, the World Cup. YWAM set up musical instruments on the streets; Joy performed with puppets, and I directed the pantomime. We would attract a crowd. Then, a team member would grab a microphone and start preaching.

After the World Cup, a few of us drove a van filled with supplies to Poland near Gliwice. This was during martial law, and tanks opposing solidarity were seen rolling up and down the streets. Despite the political situation, a Catholic youth camp was meeting at and helping to renovate a run-down palace outside a small village called Pławniowice. Joy and I decided to help with some of the renovations for a few weeks. So, we headed to the Polish countryside to work on an old German palace with a Polish youth group. We still have a drawing of this palace because one of Joy's roommates was an architectural student and had sketched the building. The Pławniowice Palace and its balcony played an important role in the story of our budding relationship. There we were, two young Americans sitting on this romantic balcony in the Polish countryside. We had been warned against forming

relationships with the participants of a mission trip while overseas. Romantic inclinations towards a team member should be ignored. It's just culture shock. Yet, 40 years later, that "culture shock" still hasn't worn off. (Pławniowice Palace has been fully renovated and is now a tourist site.)

Life Lesson

The spiritual lesson that I learned during this phase of life had a profound impact on me. When I get an idea or thought, I learn to ask myself if it comes from me. Does it come from God? Or maybe it comes from Satan. I practiced listening to the voice of the Holy Spirit in me fully and with total trust. I started asking myself, was this missionary idea from me or was it from the Holy Spirit? Or was there something else going on? I went through an intense time (over a year) where I listened to the thoughts in my head and attempted to distinguish them as either my own thoughts, the Holy Spirit's thoughts, or even potential temptation from Satan. I learned to pray out loud and then listen for the will of God.

2 Corinthians 10:5 "Take captive every thought to make it obedient to Christ." (NIV)

I was getting a message that something else was going on. Missions, yes. Architecture, no.

I never pursued a career in architecture, but I still have a deep appreciation for it. Whenever I come across a well-designed building, I can't help but admire it. I have a particular fondness for beautifully designed churches, especially Lutheran and Episcopal churches. On Sundays, I drop off Joy at our church for worship band rehearsal and then head to the Episcopal Church for their early morning service. The view of Pagosa Peak from the middle of the church in the early morning is simply breathtaking. The morning sunlight fills the interior of the church with a warm glow, and the reflection of the 11,000-foot mountain adds to the beauty of the space. It feels like the interior of the church is perfectly designed to showcase this stunning view. Instead of just focusing on the liturgy or worship music, it feels like a direct celebration of God as the creator of such majestic beauty, and we respond with gratitude in our worship.

Life in Berlin, Germany

The Engagement Story

As Joy and I celebrated Thanksgiving in 2023 with family and friends, I told our engagement story, which began exactly 40 years ago. Joy's birthday is on November 24th (Thanksgiving Day in 1983), so I targeted that date for the proposal. A couple of things preceded this event. How did I know she was the right one? It was probably the only time in my life that I almost actually heard the voice of God.

I was visiting Joy during fall break at her Louisiana home, and we were already romantically inclined. We were sitting on her bed, talking and kissing. That is when I believed I heard a direct statement from the throne. "She's the one." I pulled back. Whoa! Does that mean what I think it means?

My own mother, who was a prayer warrior, said to me one day, "You know, I've been praying about you and Joy; you know she's the one." "Yes, I know" I replied. My mother continued, "She's the one, and I just want to make sure that you know that." My mother kind of had this direct line to the throne of heaven.

After the ORU summer mission team of 1983, Joy and I stayed in Germany and were each living in a tiny room in a Studentenwohnheim (student housing) in Berlin. Each room was one twin bed wide and two twin beds long. It had a bed, a desk, and a Schrank (an armoire) in which to hang our clothes. Joy was enrolled in the Freie University, located in southern Berlin. I enrolled in the Technical University (TU), in Berlin, to study architecture. I hated it because the TU only produces what the United States calls architectural engineers, known for developing off-the-shelf designs with no creativity. Functionally very correct. The plumbing works, the electricity and lights work, but the end product showed no creativity.

The students in the building shared the kitchen facilities. One night, Joy boiled chicken and vegetables for me. I thought, "Oh, this is good. She can cook." Well, little did I know that this meal was the only thing she could cook. Obviously, she's improved since then. I taught her a little bit about spices. I'll never forget the day she made soup with beans in it. I'll eat anything. However, when she served the soup, the beans were as hard as stones. Oops! She didn't know that type of bean had to be soaked first.

The enchanting story of our engagement begins a couple of weeks before Joy's birthday. It was a few weeks before Thanksgiving when I embarked on a period of fasting, believing that the decision to marry is the second most important decision one can make, with salvation being the foremost. This belief led me to approach this decision with the utmost solemnity. As we were working with the Südstern Church in Berlin, I sought and obtained the key to the church from one of the pastors. The church building was steeped in history, particularly due to its association with Kaiser Wilhelm (Emperor William the Second). Many visitors to Berlin are familiar with the bombed-out church in the heart of Kurfürstendamm, which was named after Kaiser Wilhelm. Within the Südstern Church, there were two high-back chairs made of solid oak, which were believed to have been used by the emperor himself. I arranged these two chairs in front of the altar as part of my plan.

I had carefully selected a unique engagement ring for Joy, which featured three rubies, each separated by two delicate diamonds. The symbolism was profound; the rubies represented the Father, Son, and Holy Spirit, with the two diamonds signifying the two of us, nestled in the middle. When the time came, I seated Joy in one of the Kaiser chairs, presented the ring to her, and awaited her reaction. Her initial response was one of surprise, curiosity and an inquisitive expression. I proceeded to express my heartfelt intentions, saying, "Joy Miller, by the power of the Holy Spirit and with my unwavering commitment to cherish you for the rest of my life, will you marry me?"

Her response was quintessentially Joy – she looked into my eyes and uttered a simple, "Uh huh." For us, "uh huh" became the cherished and accepted equivalent of "yes" in our household. Afterward, we took the subway to Southwest Berlin, the location of many American military families. We had been invited to a Thanksgiving dinner hosted by a military family from the church. Approximately 20 Americans gathered there on that day. Joy was just beaming and showing everyone her ring. The Thanksgiving party topped off our engagement celebration.

Count Michael Marx

Believe it or not, my siblings and I are royalty. You could call me Graf Michael Joseph Marx, my brother Graf Alfred Joseph Michael Marx, and my sister Gräfin Helen Elizabeth Mary Katherine Marx III, meaning my siblings and I are aristocrats. According to some European standards, a quarter of a quarter (12.5%) entitles us to use our designations in front of our names.

There are two ways to become aristocracy: either by ancestry or by service to the nation. In our case, we qualify on both fronts. There is some long-lost link in our ancestry to Anna Maria Teresa of the Austrian Hungarian Empire. She was a beloved Empress who one of our forefathers married, the latter of whom was St. Stephen, Saint Istvan Maximillian IV. The Palffys were designated as royalty because of this newest addition of Empress Anna Maria Teresa of the Holy Roman Empire.

The Palffys were on our mother's side. They were landowners and had vineyards in the Austrian Hungarian Empire, which is now Hungary and Romania. The Palffys were well respected, and their employees found them good to work for. The workers earned a decent wage and stayed with them for years. If you read human history, that was a big deal. Transylvania, a geographical location within this area, was the home of Count (Graf) Von Dracula, a contemporary of our great-great-grandfather. It is safe to say that they were probably good friends. Would you like to admire my incisors?

While we were living in Germany, the German government decided that they would compensate entitled landowners for lost property during World War II to the tune of over $1,000 a month. Since we were 12.5 percent aristocracy, I decided to apply for compensation. I went to the appropriate landowner's office with a stack of documents, including books showing pictures of Grandfather Max–Count Maximilian–shooting at the Turks. Not only did my ancestors own a lot of land, but they also defended their home country. We were indeed eligible to make a claim. In the true sense of 'title,' we have titles, and I had documented proof.

My claim was turned down. Since I was now a citizen of a country that had more money than Germany, they refused to give me $1,000 a month. The compensation was designated for people such as displaced Polish, Bohemian, and German citizens. Even though I never got any money from the deal, it was kind of fun gathering the documentation and trying to collect it.

My mother, Edith Marx, wrote her autobiography called *The Hedge*, co-written with my father. In it, Mom talks about World War II and growing up in a palatial environment. Around 1987, Mom got a letter from the Romanian government informing her that her ancestors owned a 26-room building in the city center of Timișoara, which is classified as a palace. Mom sent me the paperwork. The government wanted us to take ownership of it, renovate it, and throw Western money at this dilapidated Eastern European building. As a 26-year-old, I tried to do math on this, and it did not look feasible. The irony in this deal was who was using the palace. It had been occupied by the tax authority (the IRS) of Romania.

Occasionally, when in Europe, I still have fun with our heritage. When my Hungarian cousins introduced me, they said, "This is our cousin from the United States." People nod a polite hello and welcome. I say, "My name is Michael Marx," and they turn their nose up at the name Marx. People in Eastern Europe are no longer impressed with that name. Invariably, my cousin Istvan then introduces me as Graf Michael Marx von Palffy. Now, when Istvan introduces me to someone in Slovakia or Austria as a Palffy, people get all wide-eyed and rub me like I was a lucky pony in the circus. It's terribly embarrassing, but it's worth a chuckle. Istvan enjoys watching me become embarrassed because he is a rascal.

This entire financial compensation story was more about validating our lineage. Everyone in Europe knows that the aristocracy in World War I and II has been largely compensated for their losses. My story, more than anything, validates the title. According to the European Union protocol of titles and lineage, technically, I could walk off an airplane and say, "Please call me Count Michael."

Joy, the Chicken & the Wooden Leg

Once upon a time, there was a wooden leg. It belonged to my grandmother, on my mother's side.

In December 1983, I made plans to travel to Romania to visit my grandmother, also known as Aunt Esti. Technically she wasn't my grandmother, but rather my grandmother's sister, who raised my mother for several years. One of the things that Mom wanted, for whatever reason, was her mother's wooden leg. 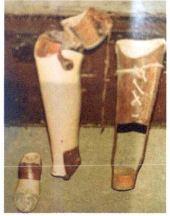 She had previously visited her mother/aunt in Timișoara, Romania, and she knew exactly where it was in the attic. I had specific directions on how to find it. My biological grandmother had been a young 'Gräfin,' a countess with one leg because she had been run over by a streetcar in Timișoara.

Joy and I booked a trip to Bucharest and arrived on Christmas Eve. One of my objectives was to dispel the image of Transylvania being a scary place. However, Hollywood doesn't do this place justice. It is much scarier than Hollywood depicts. In the movies, it is always very dark, and everyone is walking around with their collars pulled over their ears amid a swirling, thick, orangish fog. Yes, that was exactly the way it looked. It was scary.

We finally found an (unofficial) taxi driver. With seven or eight bars of chocolate, we were able to bribe him to take us to my grandmother's house. Esti was thrilled at our arrival.

Esti had saved for weeks to get a fresh chicken to serve on Christmas. Remember, this was still during the communist era in Romania. We offered to help her with the preparation of her chicken. My grandmother handed Joy the chicken feet. Unfortunately, Joy had no idea what she was expected to do with them. My fiancée and my grandmother were speaking German, so communication wasn't the problem. Grandma then said, "What kind of woman are you? You don't even know how to prepare a chicken?" This was one of those moments of mortification that I'll remember forever. Joy just told her she had no idea what to do with the feet. My grandmother did it for her while Joy followed her lead.

Then we talked about Mom and Pop and our family. The conversation eventually turned to the wooden leg. We asked if we could find it. Esti said, "You don't want that!" I said, "No, I don't want it, but my mother does." Sure enough, I readily found the leg, almost in the exact spot Mom had described.

So, I retrieved the wooden leg, took it to North Carolina, and gave it to Mom. I don't know what she did with it. She didn't get $1,000 a month for restitution, but she got the wooden leg.

The H Story

My mother immigrated from Europe after World War II and followed the process to become a U.S. citizen. After living in the country for the requisite number of years, she applied for citizenship at the U.S. Immigration office in Manhattan, NY. She had to study U.S. history and go through an interview process. The interviewer reviewed Mom's paperwork and saw the last name of Marx and her birthday. He then asked for her first name, to which she replied, "Edith." "Give me your middle name." "I don't have one," which is typical for Europeans of that era. Most Europeans from the 20s through the 80s do not have a middle name.

I have been on airplanes with Europeans who have suddenly gotten flustered while filling out their customs paperwork. There's a mandatory spot on the form for a middle name. That's when I told them the story of my mother immigrating to the United States. Mom provided her last name and her first name and stated that she didn't have a middle name. The immigration officer looked at her and said, "We have to have a middle name." Mom relents and says, "H." The immigration officer said that she couldn't have H as a middle name. She retorted, "Yes, I can." He said, "No, you can't. Does it mean Helen? Does it mean Hildegarde? What does 'H' mean?" She said, "H means H. The president of the United States is Harry S. Truman, and S means S. It doesn't stand for Sam or Stuart. It is just Harry S. Truman. The immigration officer looked at her and told her that with that answer, she could have H. I have always considered it quite amusing how this spunky little 5'2" lady stood up to U.S. Immigrations.

The Wedding

 Joy and I were married on March 17, 1984, in Louisiana. In preparation for this special event, Joy returned to the USA a couple of months in advance to prepare. She made all the flower arrangements out of silk flowers. She didn't even buy a new wedding dress but opted instead to rent a white wedding dress from a theater costume shop in Berlin. I was terribly impressed with Joy renting her dress and mused, "I like this girl. She isn't spending thousands of dollars on a wedding dress which will only be used once." The sweet little old lady in the shop only charged her the weekend rental rate even though Joy kept the dress for two months. Her main "fee" was a picture of our wedding.

I embarked on a remarkable journey, driving from the charming state of North Carolina to the vibrant state of Louisiana just a week after returning from our future home together in Berlin. At the age of 22, I was filled with anticipation and joy as I was about to enter the sacred bond of marriage. The 17-hour drive seemed like a monumental feat, considering it was my first time covering such a long distance without a break. However, my eagerness to reach my destination overshadowed any fatigue, and I was overjoyed upon finally arriving.

As an eager, young couple, Joy and I had taken it upon ourselves to delve into literature about marriage, seeking wisdom and guidance. Two books stood out as valuable resources: *Two Shall Become One* by John and Rymier Mann, and *Intended for Pleasure* by Ed Wheat, a candid guide tailored for Christian married couples.

Our wedding ceremony was a truly unforgettable affair. We chose to compose and recite our own vows, which, in the whirlwind of emotions, proved to be a challenging yet deeply meaningful experience. What made our ceremony truly unique was the heartfelt exchange of songs between us. It remains a treasured memory, especially considering that it may very well have been the only instance in my life when I sang a solo, a gesture I made solely for our wedding.

One of the most vivid memories from our special day was the delightful chaos surrounding the wedding cake. With all the wedding preparations masterfully handled by Joy, my only fervent request (or rather, demand) was for a moist wedding cake. I had encountered many visually stunning yet disappointingly dry cakes at previous events, and I was resolute in ensuring that ours would not suffer the same fate. And indeed, our cake was a delectable triumph! Upon arriving at the reception, I was greeted by the sight of my sister standing beside the magnificent multi-tiered cake, a knife anxiously lodged into its side to prevent its imminent collapse. Her urgent gaze and commanding tone left no room for negotiation as she declared, "You're going to cut the cake, NOW."

With that, our plans were swiftly altered to accommodate the pressing matter at hand, and we joyfully proceeded to cut the cake, marking the beginning of a new chapter in our lives.

I also remember that the minister had the marriage certificate prepared for signatures. One of the witnesses to sign the document was Joy's grandfather, who was the stalwart epitome of a good Christian father and gentleman. Joy seriously loved her grandfather. I loved her grandfather. One of Gran's hobbies was repairing watches and clocks. As I sit here in my office today (2023), I'm staring at a grandfather clock that needs repair. Gran inspired me to become a grandfather clock repairman, and I still have that aspiration.

On our way to our first home together in Berlin, we went on a skiing honeymoon in Switzerland. Skiing has been a pivotal part of our lives together.

> *Joy:* At the time, we could never have guessed how Michael's passion for skiing would influence and shape the rest of our lives. Going on yearly ski trips to Switzerland solidified my passion. After specializing in ski trips for a Louisiana travel agency, we lived in a Colorado ski area for a couple of years in the 90's. Upon returning to Germany, I established a business called America Ski & Sun specializing in sending German clients to North America for ski vacations.

Newlyweds in Berlin

Following our honeymoon, we returned to Berlin. While Joy had been stateside preparing for the wedding, I was in Berlin preparing our first apartment. Berlin is architecturally interesting. I enjoyed looking at old (pre-World War II) architecture in Berlin. The apartment buildings of that era ranged from four to six stories high; they each had a stairwell and a basement.

Our first apartment was in the district of Wedding (the northern section of West Berlin), which I thought was rather amusing following our wedding. The building was so old the individual apartments were heated by a ceramic coal oven located in the living room. Ceramic ovens burned bricks of coal, which were each about eight inches long and two inches thick. Every Sunday, I made it a ritual to go to the basement and cart 50 bricks from the basement up to our apartment on the fifth floor so that we would have heat. Two years after moving to this apartment, the management decided to upgrade the heating system and increase the rent. Since we were not in favor of paying more rent ($150 a month), we decided to move to a different apartment in the same area.

Beneath our new apartment was a Yugoslavian restaurant, which became one of our favorite restaurants. The Berlin Wall was located no more than 100 yards from our front door. Our living room window and bedroom balcony overlooked no man's land.

At the time, I was preparing to run the Berlin marathon. Since the Berlin Wall was outside my front door, I was able to do my long-distance training alongside the wall since it stretched on indefinitely. Normally, when you're running long distances in the middle of a city, you're always coming to intersections where you must stop and wait to cross, hopefully without getting run over. Running along the Berlin Wall was great as there were no intersections.

We lived in Berlin from 1983 until 1989. Berlin is one of the most fascinating cities in the world, but it is also a place of high tension. When we lived in Berlin, we noticed that the closer you got to the wall when driving or walking down the streets, the more nervous people became. People were more erratic in their driving styles. They were more aggressive in their communication styles. The Berlin Wall not only had a serious political impact on the city, but it had a serious mental impact. (Sidenote: The Berlin Wall fell in November 1989, just a few months after we moved back to the USA.)

One of the other interesting things about the district of Wedding was the nearby subway stop. This line went under Berlin Mitte, which was the central district of Russian-occupied East Berlin. On Sunday mornings, we would take the subway under East Berlin and come out on the other side into the southern section of West Berlin. Those original subway stops in East Berlin were closed and always manned by armed East German guards. Due to the subway under East Berlin, we could get to our church relatively easily. The Südstern church was our primary place of socialization, where we were involved in theater, street outreaches, and puppet ministry. During our Berlin years, we both taught English for the Berlitz School of Languages.

When we adopted our first dog, Cindy, we quickly realized she was unique and amazing. Cindy was smart, attentive, affectionate, personable, and everyone loved her. However, living on the fifth floor of an apartment building presented a unique challenge when Cindy needed to go outside for her business. Every morning, one of us would take Cindy down the stairs to the green area in front of the building before heading to work. Afterwards, that person would let Cindy back into the building, and she would run all the way up the five stories and back into the apartment. It was truly incredible.

We took Cindy everywhere. We took her to church, restaurants,

and to work. Once, we even took her to Club Aldiana, an all-inclusive vacation hotel, where we gave her a role in a couple of our pantomimes. She also accompanied us on our ski vacations. Joy purchased a front-load baby carrier to transport her on the ski lift. At the top, she jumped out and ran down the mountain behind us. Cindy was incredibly well-behaved. She was like our test run for parenting, and she exceeded all our expectations. Consequently, when we eventually adopted a child who didn't always listen to us, we were surprised.

One day, as I was reading an article from Time Magazine, I couldn't help but blurt out, "Joy, we've been classified!" Apparently, couples in their twenties and thirties without children but with a dog were being referred to as DINKS, which stood for dual income/no kids.

Club Aldiana

One of the more fun things Joy and I did together was to go to a club-like hotel that offered all-inclusive stays for German guests who wanted to be highly catered to. Club Aldiana is in various Mediterranean countries, such as Crete, Turkey, and the Canary Islands. Guests would enjoy amenities such as water skiing, dancing, painting, and English lessons. The Club hired the Berlitz School of Languages–the company we worked for in Germany–to teach English for 90 minutes per day to the guests in exchange for a four-week paid vacation. Additionally, since we both had a love for drama, we also volunteered to be part of the entertainment crew participating in the evening shows as actors. As part of the entertainment and educational staff, we had to be ready to serve Monday through Saturday, leaving free time on Sunday. Sometimes we would rent a car and explore the area. Our visit to the ruins of Ephesus in Turkey was especially impressive. One time I clearly remember renting dirt bikes and exploring around the island of Crete. Due to her inexperience driving in sand, Joy lost traction and landed in the sand. Her full, curly hair was encrusted in dust! It was hilarious.

During our travels in Turkey, Crete, and Italy, we had the pleasure of indulging in the exquisite flavors of Mediterranean cuisine. One culinary delight that impressed Joy was the abundance of succulent shrimp piled high on platters. As for me, I was enamored with the delectable stuffed grape leaves, a delicacy that I simply couldn't get enough of. Additionally, my fondness for hummus grew, and it remains one of my all-time favorite snacks. I take pride in crafting my own hummus, and I must say, I do a pretty good job at it. However, I confess that Joy's stuffed grape leaves are truly unparalleled and undoubtedly the best in the world.

Back in the USA

MBA and Youth Pastor

After spending six years in Berlin, my wife and I decided to return to the USA in 1989 so that I could pursue a Master of Business Administration. I enrolled in the MBA program at Northeast Louisiana University, now known as the University of Louisiana at Monroe, and successfully completed the program in two years, earning my MBA. During this time, Joy worked at a travel agency, where she specialized in ski packages due to her extensive experience with skiing and resorts, while I dedicated myself to my studies. As a graduate student, I was also given the opportunity to teach. Thanks to my prior teaching experience and my studies of art and architecture in Berlin, I was appointed to teach Art Appreciation, a role that I found immensely fulfilling as I delved into the works of popular artists such as Van Gogh and Monet.

One Sunday, shortly after we started attending Pine Grove Church, the pastor announced that the church was looking for a new youth minister. Despite initially dismissing the idea and driving home after the service, I felt strongly compelled to return to the church to discuss the youth pastor position. I encountered the two lead pastors, the only people remaining in the building by that time. After introducing myself, I shared that I felt compelled to talk to them about the youth ministry. All of us were astounded as they described their prayer and impression that the Lord would show them that very day who was to become the next youth ministry leader. Consequently, I became the youth minister of Pine Grove Church in 1989, a role for which I had no formal training, inclination, or resources. Despite the challenges, I embraced the position wholeheartedly, finding it to be a rewarding and enjoyable experience. Over the course of three years, I gained valuable insights into working with teenagers and honed my leadership skills.

> *Joy:* Before our move to Louisiana, I had a strong impression that Michael should be a youth pastor while pursuing his studies. Although I can't recall if I shared this with Michael at the time, the sequence of events leading to his role as a youth minister has always left me in awe of God's guidance.

Milton

We began pursuing our next life goal, which involved adopting a child – a significant event for us. Joy's stepfather, Herb, had a background as a chemical engineer specializing in bleaching textiles and paper. After retiring, he worked as a consultant, occasionally traveling to South America to oversee bleaching system installations. Joy's mother, Judy,  accompanied Herb on some of his longer trips, including one to Chile. During their time in Chile, Judy befriended a woman whose older daughter was a lawyer, and whose younger daughter,

Carmen, was in law school. Carmen, along with her sister and mother, played a pivotal role in connecting us with an orphanage in Chile, as we had expressed our wish to adopt a girl. I distinctly recall Carmen calling us one evening to inform us that we had a choice to adopt a two-year-old girl along with her four-year-old brother or to adopt a six-year-old boy. It was 9 o'clock at night, and we had until 11 pm to make our decision. We reached out to our church's prayer chain, our parents, and others for intense prayers to guide us in making the right decision. Soon, we made our choice and called Carmen back to inform her that we would be adopting the six-year-old boy. His name was Milton Sebastian Betancur-Toledo, which is a common naming convention in South America, where two last names with a hyphen are used, with the first last name being the father's last name and the second last name being the mother's surname. We traveled to Chile to work with Carmen on Milton's adoption, and the entire process, from the initial stages until the day Milton arrived in Monroe, Louisiana, took nine months. We often refer to this period as our "pregnancy" because it involved nine months of hard labor, including demonstrating our legal intent to the Chilean government and court system, translating all the documents, and obtaining release from the birth mother. Throughout this process, we also met Milton's brother Christian, whom a neighbor had adopted. Milton and Christian remain in contact with each other and with their birth mother through Facebook. In January 1992, Milton arrived in Monroe, Louisiana, and he was just as adorable and personable as one could imagine. Upon arriving in the United

States, he was welcomed with a room full of toys and his own bed. One of his favorite things was a shallow splash pool, which he would play in for hours, especially during the hot Louisiana summer. Watching him play in the pool brought us immense joy. Cindy, our dog, also enjoyed playing with him in the pool. Milton cherished his time with Cindy, and observing the two of them playing together was truly heartwarming. Everyone from Pine Grove Church appeared to be very interested in the whole process of adopting this six-year-old from a Chilean orphanage. Consequently, whenever Milton showed up with us, the church would get energized, and old ladies would cry. Milton began making friends with the children at the church. At that time, some children in Pine Grove were getting baptized, so Milton decided that he wanted to be baptized too. Joy and I talked about his name and recognized that it would be a good time to change it if Milton so desired since a baptismal certificate is considered a legal document. I think this is a funny story:

Since I was still in graduate school, I was taking care of Milton during the day. We managed even though his operative language was still Spanish. Joy knew some Spanish, but I knew none. From my six-year-old, I learned some of the important words like la piscina (swimming pool). One day I got a letter in the mail addressed to Michael Joseph Marx. Milton picked up the envelope, looked at it, and saw the first name Michael. Okay. And then he saw Joseph, and I said, "That's my middle name. Do you like my middle name?" He agreed that he did like it. I said, "Do you like your middle name? Sebastian?" He said, "No. No me gusta, Sebastian." So, in my broken Spanish, I said, "Well, Milton, we'll let you change your name if you want to change your name. Milton is your first name. What about Sebastian? Do you want to change your middle name?" And he said, "Sí, sí." I said, "What would you like your new middle name to be?" He was staring at this envelope and holding it with both hands but not responding. I thought that perhaps he didn't understand the question. Then, suddenly, his eyes got big. And he said, "Yo sé, (I know) Pinocchio."

We hoped that he would forget. A few weeks later, we asked him again what he wanted as his middle name. He said, "Pinocchio." And we thought, oh shoot, he hasn't forgotten. We explained to him that he couldn't choose Pinocchio. He said, "Okay, Joy." "Well, no, that doesn't work either. You can choose Michael, though." And that is what he did. His name is now Milton Michael Marx. I always thought the Pinocchio story was funny!

Return to Germany

When we left Germany in 1989, we had planned to return to Germany within a couple of years. One of the denomination leaders asked me to be their Business Director. I didn't feel qualified for that, which is one of the reasons I pursued the MBA (Master of Business Administration). I wanted to be able to effectively lead a denomination including all aspects of business, administration, and leadership. After receiving my master's degree, we moved to Gunnison, Colorado (1992) for a couple of years. Finally, in 1995, we felt it was time to move back to Germany to pursue our calling, this time not in Berlin but rather in Hanover. I began teaching primarily business English. Joy started a travel agency (America Ski & Sun) that specialized in sending Germans to ski resorts in the Rockies.

The church was an integral part of our lives and our main reason for living in Germany. I had planned to be the business leader but was asked to take over the position of lead pastor.

> ***Detlef & Alexandra:*** Thank you, Michael and Joy for having given yourselves as missionaries to Germany. You were not only our pastor, but our dear friends as well. Michael will leave a gap in our lives until we meet in eternity.

Starting in 2000, I became a full-time professor for two different colleges. One was the community college where I was teaching

English as a Second Language (ESL), and the second one was a computer school where most of my students were programmers learning English from me. During that time, hip-hop music was becoming popular. To relate to my students, I used the hip-hop mindset to teach my lessons in a way that would relate to a computer programmer's learning style. That's a challenge right there.

At that time, we also actively pursued the life goal of owning our own home. We purchased a single-story house with a flat roof, known in Germany as a bungalow. There were seven bungalows close together in our neighborhood.

Each year, we hosted a fourth of July party, which became a big neighborhood event. It started with just 30 people, and the last party had around 300 people attending. We soon discovered that we were helping to break down cultural barriers that had existed for decades. I still look back fondly on those days when Germans got to know each other. As it is indicative of many cultures, including Northern Germany, people didn't transition from last names to first names until about two or three years into the relationship. I remember that at our Fourth of July parties, all the neighbors sat around the same table and Joy was chatting with them. I was standing 10 or 15 feet away, and Joy asked the oldest person at the table, "So how long do we have to be neighbors until we go from last name to first name?" The whole table went stone-faced because Joy was too young to ask that question. The oldest person at the table was more than 80 years old. He was the one who should have started the switch from last names to first names. He looked at her, and he answered, "17 years, and that ends today." He held his hand out to Joy and said, "My name is Horst." I understood the significance of what was unfolding, so I raced over there and said, "Hello, Horst, my name is Michael," and shook his hand. Then all the neighbors shook hands for the first time in 17 years and shared their first names. It was surreal for these people who have lived next door to each other for all these years not to acknowledge each other's first names. From that point forward, the neighborhood was on a first-name basis.

The Fourth of July party was an American-style party. Bring food and share with all. At our party, the invitation said to bring your own meat, so people would bring their own meat, and a few of us would cook it on the grill. We had three or four grills, which was strange for a lot of them.

My sister was the first person that piled grilled meat on a tray and started passing it out indiscriminately to whoever was sitting at the tables. People would look at the tray passing by them and think, "Oh, there's my steak. What is she doing with my steak? She's taking my steak to the other side of the property." Sorry! It's an American party. Get used to it!

Our dog Cindy loved our events because everybody kept dropping pieces of meat on the ground. She was even bold enough to steal a hot steak from the top of one of the grills. A neighbor approached me and said, "Your dog stole my steak from the grill." I said, "Are you saying that my dog jumped up on the grill and stole your steak off of a hot grill?" He said, "That's exactly what I'm telling you!" That was our Cindy, and I don't think anybody minded in the end.

Bier

The Germans take great pride in their local beer, which is often brewed at nearby breweries and is commonly known as pils or pilsner beer. This pale lager is highly regarded, especially in the northern German states where preservatives are frowned upon. The emphasis on freshness means that local beer has a short shelf life to preserve its distinct flavor.

In my experience, Germans can be described as quite proud, or some might say "arrogant," when it comes to their local beers. I once conducted a taste test in Hannover, challenging my economics class to distinguish between various beers in a double-blind experiment. To their surprise, the students couldn't differentiate between a cheap local beer and a relatively expensive one, prompting some reconsideration of their assumptions.

Beer-making in Germany is steeped in tradition, with a preference for older recipes believed to produce superior beer. For example, the oldest beer recipe in the world hails from Prague, Czech Republic, and American Budweiser is brewed according to this

Czech recipe. Germans take pride in beers brewed from centuries-old recipes, which can be a fascinating but also a curious aspect of their beer culture.

As for my personal preference, I enjoy beers with a robust malt flavor, and I'm partial to amber ales. I find it amusing that German export beers are often labeled as lager, which translates to "storage" in English. It's worth noting that these beers are designed to withstand long journeys, making them some of the oldest beers available once they reach their destination.

Additionally, Germany offers a variety of interesting beer mixtures, such as the popular "Spritz" made by mixing beer with Sprite, or "Sholle" made with orange soda. There are also pre-mixed lemon soda options called Radler or Alsterwasser, as well as the unique Berliner Weisse, which is flavored with syrups, most commonly pine syrup. This beer is quite distinctive, as it has a dominant pine syrup flavor rather than a traditional beer taste. Lastly, Germans also enjoy spiced Christmas beers, which are commonly served at Christmas markets in various flavors and blends.

Don't go to the Oktoberfest

Oktoberfest in everyone's mind—German and non-German—is the epitome of getting down and dirty, a surreal experience. Some people think that it is the most fun beer party in the world. Michael Marx thinks it is the least fun party in the world. I have never seen Germans nastier, more pushy, more belligerent, less friendly, and less congenial than in an Oktoberfest beer tent. If you think you are going to get from one side of a pavilion (tent) to another with a Fassbrause, a liter-sized glass of beer, you are probably going to be wearing it. Fassbrause is also known as keg soda and is a traditional German drink made from fruit and malt extract.

Brats and Brötchen

Along with beer goes a requisite eight-inch-long sausage called a Bratwurst, nicknamed brat. To truly experience a beer, you must have a brat with plain yellow mustard. German's arrogance towards local beer is only exceeded by their pride and arrogance in what is known as Brötchen, a hard roll about the size of a flattened orange. In my opinion, there is a Brötchen in every country in the world. In France, it is a baguette. In Greece - a koulouria. In Mexico - a tortilla. In Italy - a panini. In the United States, we have sandwich bread. Every country has a version of this icky, nutritionally worthless white bread.

When eating Bratwurst, put it on a Brötchen and add yellow mustard. On Fridays, serve it on a Brötchen and smother it with curry ketchup for a Currywurst tradition. The ketchup is served warm and absolutely smothered in curry powder.

The first time I went to a currywurst booth in Berlin and wanted to get a wurst, I held up my index finger (a normal American gesture) with my palm facing my nose and said, "Ein Currywurst bitte." The man pushing this cart said, "Zwei?" I repeated, "Ein Currywurst bitte." He replied, "Zwei?" Again, I repeated, "Ein currywurst bitte." He replied, "Zwei?" I'm thinking, this is not working at all. So, I bought two currywurst. Now, that was a hard-working joke, but it is repeated every day when an American touches down in Germany, this finger thing. In other words, you must know that only the thumb indicates one item, and any more fingers than that will get you two or three or four or five.

A Wedding & a Tag

Written by Elizabeth, Michael's sister

On January 30, 2003, we all congregated in Minneapolis for Fred and Lisa's wedding. Michael was stranded in Amsterdam for an additional 24 hours and missed the pre-wedding festivities. The next day, Michael arrived jetlagged, without luggage or anything to wear to the

wedding. He had the clothes on his back, his traveling shoes, and the blue booties that KLM gave him. What a day! We had to dash out to the Mall of America, where we bought a suit, shirt, and tie. He kept the KLM booties and the travel shoes on, though.

Dressed and ready to go, we discovered that Michael still had the ink-loaded security tag fastened to his suit pants, and there was nothing we could do to remove it. We arrived at the church on time but frazzled. The family pictures featured a bright yellow plastic ink tag and lots of laughter!

Over the years, it seemed that each time Michael and I got together, something would go amuck. We left expensive tickets to a Broadway play in a phone booth in Times Square, forgot a bag with his purchases in New Jersey, confused the meeting spot in Frankfurt, thus missing each other. But somehow, we always found our way back to each other to laugh about our memorable adventures!

Ode to Joy & a Flute

Many people give extravagant gifts to their loved ones for Valentine's Day. They buy unique things like a spot on the ocean floor, a piece of history, a star, or even a moon crater.

For my superstar wife, a ski slope in British Columbia is now named "Ode to Joy." As their travel agent, Joy had arranged a helicopter skiing trip for a group of German dentists and me to Canada at Tyax Lodge & Heliskiing. The Tyax area boasts unlimited vertical heliskiing. Occasionally, the helicopter flies the group to an uncharted slope, which had never been skied before. One day the guide led us to ski down such a slope of untouched snow, and I was the first to make it down safely. I was allowed to name that run "Ode to Joy" after my wife. We skied multiple virgin runs that day, and we all agreed to name one slope in her honor.

My wife Joy is a talented flutist whose silver open-hole flute was stolen. Like any musician, Joy had an emotional attachment to that flute and mourned its loss. After the insurance company paid the claim, Joy purchased a much cheaper soprano flute and used the remaining funds to buy an alto flute. However, she missed her old flute, so I saved money each week to buy her a new soprano silver open-hole flute. It took a few years, but I was proud to do it and grateful for the discipline it took to save the money.

The big event occurred before the Christmas service. Joy keeps all three of her flutes in a flute case: her new alto flute, the inexpensive soprano flute, and a piccolo. The case even has room for a collapsible music stand.

I told the music director that I had bought Joy a new silver open-hole flute, to which the director expressed amazement. I informed him that I would put it into her flute case so that the first time she'd ever see it was when she picked it up to play for the Christmas service. The director's eyes got big, and he said, "Oh my goodness. She's never played this before, has she?" He got a little nervous. Joy had played an open-hole flute for many years, so I was sure there wouldn't be any issue trading them out. She would see the new flute for the first time when she took it out of the case during the ensemble warm-up.

We went about the task of setting up for the Christmas special, and the other musicians pulled instruments from their cases.

Joy opened the flute case and saw the new flute pieces wrapped in velvet. She had a confused look on her face and started to unfold it. When Joy saw the open-hole silver flute, she started crying. Then I started to cry, and the music director and other musicians started to cry. She lifted her new flute and played brilliantly.

I love Joy so much (tears). She has meant the world to me since we were 22 years old. Forty years married on March 17, 2024! I was so blessed when Joy was placed into my life (tears). And now, with all

that has happened with my brain and life afterward, it's just been amazing how much she has had to deal with. She's trying to keep her head above water and is doing a great job. Sometimes it's harder than others. All that has happened since August 2023 is very complicated; there are a lot of moving parts. Let's put it this way, without her, I would be totally lost.

And yet, on any given Sunday, she can march right up there to her music stand, and despite the level of complexity, she'll open her case and play her flute beautifully even now, with all the stress she's under. It doesn't matter; she can play her flute anywhere, anytime. Perfectly.

Stampeders

In 2009, I was honored to receive a Lifetime Achievement Award for my work with the Stampeders American Football Club in Hannover, Germany. This special recognition included retiring my jersey, number 61, which means that number won't be used again.

The award is given to those who showed leadership and went above and beyond the call of duty. When I joined the club, it was struggling, but I helped bring it through tough times. Over nearly a dozen years, I was one of two head coaches. I wasn't the best player. The other coach, known as "Rambo," was the superstar of the show, an effective strategist and offensive coach, although his player license was eventually revoked due to unsportsmanlike conduct. I was Mr. Nice Guy; he was Mr. Hothead. Despite our differences, we kept growing the players and the club. Every now and then, we would even win the league trophy.

> *Elizabeth:* On one visit to the United States, Michael bought a wide assortment of football equipment. We traveled to neighboring states to pick it all up. Then we had to smudge it up with dirt before packing it for travel to avoid customs taxes on new purchases. When he arrived back in Germany, it was like Christmas for the players opening their new football gear.

As a team, we enjoyed each other's company and had a great time together, doing more than just drinking beer. For instance, every Thanksgiving, Joy single-handedly hosted and fed the entire club Thanksgiving dinner. The club roasted a couple of large turkeys and prepared mashed potatoes. Joy quarterbacked the rest of the meal for over 50 people every Thanksgiving. She is an exceptional organizer.

Players would take the day off work and bring their plastic containers so they could take home turkey, sides, and desserts. It became a Thanksgiving tradition.

My Secret Dream Job

When I was four years old, I watched in awe how the city trucks would go down our road to the dump with the workers hanging onto the back of the truck. I thought it was amazing, and it looked like so much fun. Fast forward 30 years in Germany, a local radio station was offering what they called a Dream Job Day, during which you got to do the job of your dreams for one day. I thought about that and remembered that I always wanted to ride in the back of a garbage truck. So, I called the radio station, and they were unsure that they could arrange it, but within two weeks, they did. On the designated day, I got up at five in the morning to be the new boy on the crew, resplendent in a flaming orange jumpsuit and a brand-new pair of steel-toed shoes, which were required.

They put me on the crew with the newest truck in their fleet; I was very impressed to learn that each truck costs a quarter of a million dollars. Off we went to collect the morning trash in Hildesheim, Germany. We went from building to building, rolling the bins to the back of the truck, connecting them to the lifts, loading, then disconnecting the bins.

I was impressed with my co-workers; they were all very nice and friendly, and equally focused on getting the job done quickly and efficiently while leaving no trash behind. The crew took this job very seriously. In Hildesheim, it was a high-paying job. This was not a job for people who had no future aspirations and lacked commitment. These were qualified people who intended on doing this as a career. The job was not as hard on their bodies as an outsider might think when seeing them swinging heavy cans up and returning them empty. Instead, the truck was a massive robot that did all the heavy lifting. The crew just had to move the bins close enough to trigger the sensor. Then the robot arms would come down and take care of the rest.

My shift was from 6 AM to 3 PM. My body did not ache at the end of the day, nor was I repelled by the smell. Germans pride themselves in separating the trash and putting each type of trash in its proper bag so that it can be recycled appropriately. The Germans are champion recyclers.

As a publicity opportunity for the radio station, I was interviewed and the resulting exchange was posted on their website. It was fun. Would I do it again? Sure!

Pets

I vividly remember the different dogs that have been part of my life. A couple of them accompanied me through childhood. Some dogs don't live long if they are fed an improper diet or have the bad habit of chasing cars.

Cindy was our first dog as a couple, and her story has been shared. She was almost 17 years old when she passed (1985-2002.) Coaly, a black mutt born in 1995, was Milton's dog. In spite of some mental issues, Coaly was excellent at playing hide and seek with a ball. Not only could he find any ball which we hid on the property, he like to "hide" the ball for us to find...usually in the middle of the hallway.

Angel, a Golden Labrador (2006-2021), was a remarkable dog. She was intelligent, affectionate, and well-behaved. As a trained therapy dog, she and Joy visited a Senior Center in Hannover. Angel was also Joy's first "sled" dog. A retriever is not a natural puller; they are retrievers. To train Angel to pull Joy on a scooter, I had to ride a bicycle in front of her calling her name. She eventually learned to love it. In Alaska, she even enjoyed running with the sled dogs as one of Joy's leaders. Contrary to most sled dogs, Angel made it clear that running 20 miles at one time was her limit, which is just a nice beginning for an Alaskan Husky.

Angel's presence in my life inspired me to include stories about pets in my collection. They bring us joy and affection, and I believe we need these relationships in our lives. However, I hold the unpopular belief that pets may not be present in heaven. I believe that when we get to heaven, we will run into people that we knew on Earth. Having fellowship with family and friends is not the reason to be there. The purpose of Heaven is to glorify God and to enjoy him forever. Anything that comes before God and the worship of God is not in the nature of heaven.

Despite this, I recently had a dream where I was reunited with Angel. I gave her a treat, and we cuddled for a while. Was this just a dream? Was it a vision of heaven? Who cares! I was able to hug Angel again. I can imagine having experiences like that when I'm in heaven. The moment was very sweet.

Joy: Besides the above-named wonderful dogs, I have so far welcomed 36 additional dogs into the family. Each has some wonderful attributes and a unique personality. I personally believe that if God cares for the birds (Matthew 6:26), He must love dogs even more. The 25 dogs, who currently live with me, are wonderful company and a great comfort. For my dog sledding business, I wanted to give away pens with a Bible verse on it. I chose Psalms 103:22, "All God's creatures bless the Lord!" (CEB)

Ambassador Angel

Written by Joy

(Previously published as a chapter in the book called *Only God, Stories of an Extraordinary God Revealed in the Lives of Ordinary People*, compiled by Michael and Deanna Pfau)

We got our golden Labrador retriever in 2006, and I had it in mind to train Angel to be a therapy dog. She was about 10 months old at the time of this incident. One day I was taking her for a walk in our neighborhood in Germany, which had a large field with a walking trail around it. On this day, I spotted a man sitting on a bench along the trail. Angel ran up to him and as the man started petting her, we struck up a conversation. He expressed that he was depressed over his girlfriend and their relationship. We walked around the field for some time talking about that and about life in general. I went home that day and told my husband, Michael, how Angel had brought about this small connection between me and the gentleman I had just met. She had created a bridge to connect me to another person and had provided an opportunity to minister to a stranger. It just re-confirmed my desire to have her trained as a therapy dog.

Angel received her training when she was two years old. One day Angel and I along with several other therapy dog teams visited a retirement home for the first time. A group of about fifteen elderly people sat in a circle with me, along with two other ladies and five therapy dogs. Angel ran up to one elderly woman and licked her deformed hand! These are the kind of stories that Angel and I have shared. She has created a special bridge between me and others to form an initial connection. The Lord can use His creation in profound ways to touch the lives of those in need. Only God!

For Kat

(Previously published as a chapter in the book called *Only God, Stories of an Extraordinary God Revealed in the Lives of Ordinary People*, compiled by Michael and Deanna Pfau)

Michael Marx shares his family's miraculous journey to save and adopt their beloved daughter, Kat.

Meeting our daughter, Kat, is a real God story. When I was an elder in our church in Germany, the youth group was praying for a young woman named Katarina, who was half Filipino and half German. She was kind of the youth group's "project" at the time. Kat was invited to different events and eventually she came one Sunday morning. We had just hired a new youth pastor, and we asked him to preach to the entire church for the first time. In the middle of the sermon, his wife got up and left. Naturally, I thought, "This isn't good. A pastor is preaching and his wife leaves in the middle of it." But I didn't realize that Katarina had also left, and the youth pastor's wife had chased after her.

After church, certain church members asked if I would come out into the hallway and help this girl. When I got there, Kat was sitting on the floor crying and I could tell she was scared stiff. She didn't want to go home because she feared her brother. This eighteen-year-old girl told me how she was being abused and how she was scared to go home, and I thought, "Great, there's always another side to the story." When it came to teenagers talking about tragedy, I didn't really know if I believed her, because we had an adopted son from Chile, and we had gone through many emotional trials during his teen years.

We discovered that Kat had been living in the Philippines, near a bad city. When I looked it up online, I discovered that around the time she left, twenty journalists had been beheaded. So, she was in a type of environment where there were guns and that was scary for her. At that time her brother said, "Why not come to Germany? It is safe here and you can live with me." I said, "Well, if there is any truth to what she is saying, we have a responsibility to see that she's not being abused so let's get the brother over here." We called him and he came and sat down with the pastor, the youth pastor, elders, me and a few others from the church. We asked the brother, "Okay, what's going on here? Why is she behaving this way?" And he started verbally assaulting her right in front of everyone, and we all very quickly realized the story that she had told wasn't the half of it. What he was saying was twice as bad! As we were talking, I saw this image over and over in my mind of the altar in the Old Testament, where a person comes and grabs onto the altar and pleads for sanctuary. The youth pastor made it very clear to Kat's brother that his behavior was abusive and against German law. His response was, "Whatever. I am in charge, and this is the way I do things." He continued to justify himself with very obscure reasons, but after a while I said, "Look, if we offer her sanctuary, in other words, if we take her in, feed her, provide a roof over her head every night and promise that she will go to school, would you let her go?" And he said, "Oh yes! "I thought, "Whoa, that was a fast yes." Within two hours he threw everything she owned out onto the street, and they never saw each other again.

Kat was emotionally tragic. Her brother hadn't sexually abused her, but he certainly beat her up a lot and emotionally traumatized her. And he had been encouraging her for months to commit suicide. We didn't know where she was going to go, but I had to find someone in the church who would take her in. She was over eighteen, so I perfectly expected that she would just move in with some young women and go on with life, and naturally the church would watch over her. That night she stayed with the youth pastor and that same night we had a couple visiting us and I mentioned the situation to them, and they were overwhelmed with Kat's story. Their son had just left for a six-month student exchange in Colorado, so they offered to let Kat stay with them until he returned. It was kind of an empty nest because they were lonely and missed their son. So, Kat went to live with them, but she would come over to our house after school and hang out. I asked her if she wanted to go into a roommate situation and she said, "I would really like to live with a family." We didn't have room, but I figured if I moved my office into the living room, she could have my office. It was the smallest room in the house, but I showed it to her and said, "Would you consider living here?" and she said yes.

At Christmas that year, we made our usual retreat into the mountains to do nothing. We took Kat with us and as an experiment we asked, "Would you like to live with us?" She said "Okay, so what's the deal? Why do you want this? Why are you offering me a place to live with you?" I said, "Well, when my mother was about your age she came to America as a refugee after World War II, and a Catholic family took her in and kept her until she was on her feet. If that hadn't happened, she would have been hopeless because she was not able to take care of herself. This is why I am motivated to do this." Kat said, "What do you expect from me in return?" I replied, "Well one day, you can return the favor and do the same thing." She asked, "What are the rules?" I said, "Well, there are two rules: don't steal any money and always leave the toilet seat down." And she answered, "That's it?" I came back, "Yeah, that's it." There were more rules of course, but initially that was all that I could think of. Another rule was to be sure to screw the cap back on the soda pop so it wouldn't lose its fizz. That one really had her worried!

Kat came to live with us on New Year's Day. Several years later she said, "You know, it would be a lot easier (to live in the USA) if an American adopted me." We said, "Well, we can do that." I started looking into it and discovered it wasn't easy. It's impossible, because if you take in a person after the age of sixteen, they are not eligible

for citizenship. They have no special rights. Because Kat was born in the Philippines, she couldn't participate in any lottery or visa situation besides a professional visa. Her only option was to get married or to have a professional H1B visa. When I discovered this, I said to her, "You probably don't want us to go through this adoption process." She said, "Oh, yes I do!" The thing she needed was a family. Emotionally, she never had a family.

We legally adopted Kat at the age of twenty-three, and she changed her name to "Katrielle." We still call her "Kat" but it's no longer "Katarina," it's now "Katrielle," which means "my crown is God." It's the name she chose for herself. Much to my surprise, she also changed her last name to "Marx". She then chose the middle name "Angela," which was the name of the mother who initially took Kat in during the three months her son was in Colorado. I was able to share Kat's decision to choose the name "Angela" with the woman and sadly, three months later she died from cancer. Since she had never had a daughter, this was the fulfillment of her dream.

After coming to live with us, Kat finished tenth through twelfth grade. She made a complete turnaround. She became an accomplished "A" student and even won a national hip-hop competition. She wanted to further her studies beyond high school, so we helped her enroll in Abilene Christian University where she received her bachelor's degree. Then on May 6, 2016, she graduated with her master's in clinical psychology. She didn't get a degree in psychology for selfish reasons; she got the degree because she wanted to give back. She wanted to help people like her who are traumatized.

As our story unfolded over time, we were able to put the pieces together and say, "Wow, if Kat hadn't been rescued that day, things would have been very different for her." When Kat is asked how she came to live with us she says, "I was a broken child and they were broken parents, and God let us find each other." Only God!

Careers in Hannover

My life centered around teaching at various community colleges, the BIB International College, the Dr. Buhmann School, the Leibnitz Academy as well as the Hannover House of Languages. Between these, I taught anywhere from 8 to 10 lessons per day. This did not exhaust me; in fact, I found it invigorating. It would fire me up so hot that by 7 PM, I needed to go to football practice and bang heads with the boys to get my adrenaline level back down. Those years between 2000 and 2011 marked a period during which I solidified my love for teaching and my passion for student learning.

I loved it when students asked abstract or philosophical questions and when they were curious about their own self-improvement; obviously, that complements the objective of my coaching profession. I am an effective professional for helping people move forward, which is much more than just knowledge transfer. When you're a college instructor, you usually specialize in feeding your students one bit of knowledge after another. The students write it down and then are tested at the end of the semester in hopes that learning has happened. I was very excited during these 10 years to discover how to optimize teaching among college students in their 20s as well as among other older adults that I was coaching.

I would sometimes go with Joy when she attended trade shows. There was one annual trade show called The Mountain Travel Symposium (MTS) located in various ski areas in North America. Joy would sit at a table and all the vendors, ski-focused hotels, and sellers of ski services would come every ten minutes to explain what was new and improved in their location. My job was to examine all the ski slopes.

We would usually go in late March or early April and augment the trip with familiarization excursions known as family trips. For example, Park City or Beaver Creek would invite us to come to their area and become familiar with the amenities. I would ski, and Joy would look at all the condos. She always amazed me that she could remember the features of each, such as the big fireplace or the antler chandelier. We often received special attention since we were one of the very few international travel agencies attending the MTS. Upgraded rooms, free ski equipment and lift tickets. We were always treated like royalty at those events. A pretty cool gig!

The Doctorate

In 2000, I was recruited by Sabine Greve to offer English as a second language to executives in Hannover (Hannover House of Languages.) Sabine had the ability to attract the best of the best in town to join her language school faculty. She would arrange 90-minute appointments with clients at their offices to work on improving their English communication skills. I was assigned to department heads and section leaders, basically executives. In the end, I had a waiting list which the other instructors did not have. I had thought I was doing the same thing they were, so I wondered what I could be doing differently. This contemplation led me to a deep analysis of my methods and experiences. Fast forward a decade, and it became clear that the key distinction lay in my shift from a teaching style to a coaching style, which was not just instructional but profoundly personal. Instead of solely focusing on grammar rules and vocabulary, I emphasized understanding, motivation, and personal connection, ultimately creating a more enriching experience for my learners. I distinctly remember one department head, with whom I met monthly, telling me, "You know Michael, my English is improving. I'm learning how to talk to people in English. More importantly, you're the only person in a month that I can really confide in."

The quintessence of what I do when I talk with people or teach is that I listen well. I help them move towards solutions, which is the definition of coaching. Learning this about myself had a profound effect on my life as I started reading books, attending seminars, and taking university courses. Ultimately, one academic advisor commented that my style sounded like executive coaching. I clearly remember googling and researching 'executive coaching.' I was determined to get to the core of a 'learning by conversation' technique while remaining 'solution oriented.' During lunch on day with the president of a university, I was explaining this research to him. He asked, "What are you finding?" I said, "I'm not finding anything. How is it possible that there is no research on this topic?" He suggested, "You do the research; write a dissertation."

Ultimately, I enrolled in the online doctoral program for adult education (Ed.D.) at Regent University in 2006, earning my Doctor of Education in 2009.

Since I was the first one to finish in my cohort, I began advising the other members on maximizing the process. I still have a heart for people who are working on their dissertations. They are called ABD (All but Dissertation.) In other words, if all the doctoral classwork and prerequisites are completed, the student is ABD. We call a doctorate a 'terminal degree' because it's the end of the line: you have taken every course, done all the research, and

finally, you're an expert on the topic. We like to joke that when you're a doctoral student, the degree is terminal because it'll either cause you to stop or it'll kill you. By the time I 'walked' in my cap and gown, I was ready to get out of academics. It was an unbelievable day of freedom and accomplishment.

I still advise people on that process and most people will ask me if it is worth it. I would say financially, no. You will not make any more money if you have an academic Dr. in front of your name. A medical doctor, for example, has a more sought-after market value. An Ed.D. or Ph.D. doesn't really make you any more marketable. That said, there are jobs that I could only have gotten because of the doctorate.

My dissertation focused on how people learn in a communication environment versus a classroom environment or even a group environment. Returning to the original question: Why are people in a one-to-one 'communication style' lesson learning so much better than in other environments like groups and classrooms, books and workshops, and seminars or whatever? From my research, I was a little disappointed at what came out to be the dominant reason why people learn better in an intimate, aka one-to-one, learning environment. The answer seemed to be drop-dead simple. I wondered if the simplicity of my research might trivialize it. It is summarized in one word: Trust. In a one-to-one environment, trust is essential. What is the opposite of trust? Fear.

In the average adult in the Western world, there exists a deep-seated fear of making mistakes while learning. This often stems from a moment in the earlier academic years when an answered question elicited laughter from classmates. At that point, the person typically becomes afraid or embarrassed of appearing foolish.

If you can overcome that embarrassment and resolve to learn without worrying about others' perceptions—whether they think you're smart or stupid—you will learn more effectively and efficiently. That, in a nutshell, is my academic contribution to the world.

On this note, I want to recommend a book, *Mindset–The New Psychology of Success*, written by Carol Dweck, Ph.D. I have recommended this book hundreds of times to clients. I remember one client who said, "Michael, thank you for recommending *Mindset*. You're fired." I recoiled, "Excuse me?" She said, "Everything that I needed from coaching was in that book." Today, you can find a lot of material about a growth mindset on the internet and through every coach in the world. In summary, a growth mindset basically says I will make a fool of myself to stretch myself and learn, as opposed to the fixed mindset that says I can only learn in a very confined set of circumstances because that's how I learned in school.

For many years following the completion of my doctorate, I served as an associate professor in international business and international finance at Concordia University of Wisconsin in Mequon. These were online courses that had a strong following even prior to the COVID-19 pandemic when the entire university transitioned to online learning.

Now, here we are in 2023, and I have chemo brain. I am trying to train myself to overcome my own cognitive disability because of the chemo treatments that I've received over the last few months. I like it when people call me Dr. Marx. It makes me feel like some of those hundreds and hundreds of hours of advanced learning have gotten me some recognition and helped to affirm me, especially right now when I'm struggling with chemo fog.

Cathy: I feel both honored and motivated by the ways Michael has chosen to navigate this journey and share it with all of us. From my mother's experience with cancer, I've learned that 'healing' differs significantly from 'curing.' I will never again claim that someone has 'lost a battle' with cancer. Cancer does not prevail. Cancer never prevails. God's healing triumphs — regardless of how the situation may seem to us as humans.

Final Return to USA

Alaska

Upon deciding that 2012 was the right time to move back to the USA after having lived in Germany for 23 years, we had the opportunity to pick anywhere in the USA to live. We had always planned to move to Colorado. However, after much consideration, we decided not to decide. We purchased a 28' travel trailer and began a 3-year adventure of living on the road. These adventures have been shared with friends and family via Angel's Facebook page and travel blog called Travels with Angel. The (mostly picture) blog tells the story of our travels from Germany (2012)  through the USA in a travel trailer, the years in Alaska (2013-2015), our move to Colorado, and our life with the sled dogs (2015-2019.) **https://travelswithangel.wordpress.com/**

We picked the trailer up in Louisiana and drove it to Florida. During the fall of 2012, we worked our way up the East Coast, spending some time in North Carolina, where my mother was still living. We stopped off in Maryland to visit my sister and then traveled further north to visit childhood friends in New Jersey. North through Maine and into Canada. Ultimately, the goal was to end up in Anchorage, Alaska, for the beginning of the Iditarod dog sled race in March 2013. Joy volunteered and worked in five or six different departments during a five-week period. During that time, we decided to move to Fairbanks, Alaska, to work with a dog sled operation to give Joy the training and experience she needed in this new venture. Since we weren't needed until September, we made our way back to Louisiana and then returned to Alaska. We referred to ourselves as reverse snowbirds - south in the summer and north in the winter. Oh well, we have always been a bit unique.

The trip towards Fairbanks in September 2013 ended just 90 miles from our destination. Joy was driving. Our truck and trailer hit black ice and suddenly, we had no control of the steering wheel. The truck slid off the road and jackknifed, which caused the trailer to turn upside down. No one was hurt, but everything was totaled. We tried to empty the trailer as much as possible. Our friends from the dog yard came to our rescue, picking us and our belongings off the roadside after our unfortunate accident. As if the situation couldn't get any worse, we discovered that during the night, while our trailer lay precariously overturned, a small group of thieves had taken advantage of our misfortune. They rummaged through our camper, leaving it in disarray and making off with anything of value they could find.

Fortunately, the police managed to track down the culprits. In a surprising twist, they visited the home of one gang member and made a shocking discovery: our television was hidden beneath his bed. When confronted about it, he feigned ignorance, claiming he had "no idea" how it had ended up there. Despite his nonchalant attitude, it was clear that justice was on our side this time.

We arrived at the dog yard, and the musher said, "Well, I'm glad you're here because I need you for the winter. But the deal was you would bring your own housing because I don't have any housing for you." So, we went out and bought another camper. Not a brand new one again. Thankfully, the capsized camper was under warranty, and we bought another bumper-pull camper. It was 20 years old but better built and insulated. We parked this older camper in the middle of the dog yard and proceeded to spend two winters in it. Living conditions were okay; we had a bed with heated mattress pads and, ultimately, a propane heater that kept the camper at an acceptable temperature. (We kept the temperature in the trailer between 50-60° F, which was sometimes 100° warmer than the outdoor temperature.)

The Alaskan winter was merciless, plunging temperatures well below freezing, and each morning brought a new challenge. On many occasions, I would find that my clothes had become frozen and stuck to the walls of the closet, solidified by the bitter cold. Joy, however, had figured out a smarter approach to combat this frosty predicament. Each night before settling into bed, she would strategically select her outfits for the following day. With careful consideration, she'd lay them out on the kitchen table, allowing the fabric to gradually thaw and warm overnight. Meanwhile, I would groggily awaken to the daunting task of peeling my ice-encrusted clothes from the wall, a process that required both patience and a bit of strength as I wrestled with the stubborn fabric. Joy's foresight meant she could start her day comfortably while I was left to navigate the icy remnants of my wardrobe.

During the winters of 2013-2015, we learned how to dog sled, including the actual sledding, standing, balancing, and turning. We also learned how to manage and guide tours. This was a great experience for Joy as she still uses those skills every day with her dog sled business, Mountain Paws.

You might ask, "What do you do in your spare time?" One hobby that I picked up while we were living in Germany was sandstone sculpting. Sandstone is easier to work with than granite. I started sculpting a fountain. I can imagine ultimately fitting pieces together into a kind of serenity pool, a little water fountain spilling its water into its lower tiers. While we were in Alaska, I tried my hand at ice sculpting. The bear I sculpted only lasted until spring.

During this period, I was an online professor teaching International Business and Finance part-time for Concordia University and full-time for Liberty University, which is where I met Steve Schaffer.

Steve Schaffer's Letter:

Michael stands as one of the most profound influences in my life. I embarked on my journey at Liberty University when I was 47 years old, diving into the world of online education. About six years into this transformative experience, I found myself enrolled in an International Business class. Little did I know this class would change the trajectory of my academic and spiritual life.

Dr. Marx, our professor, dedicated significant time to clarifying the expectations for our written assignments. He was thorough and precise, ensuring that we understood the importance of structure and academic integrity. When it came time to submit my first paper, I poured my heart and soul into it, meticulously following his guidelines and conducting extensive research. I confidently turned it in on time, eager to receive feedback.

However, my anticipation quickly turned to disbelief when I received my grade—a shocking "F." Flipping through the comments, I found a brief note stating, "Plagiarism." I had never encountered such a harsh response before, and anger consumed me. My poor wife bore the brunt of my frustration as I fumed about the perceived injustice. Sleep eluded me as I replayed the situation in my mind, contemplating my next steps. Finally, after what felt like an eternity of stewing, I decided to reach out to Dr. Marx via email.

What followed was a flurry of emails from me, filled with confusion and indignation, each met with Dr. Marx's calm and succinct replies. Perhaps weary of our back-and-forth, he suggested we have a phone conversation—a rarity in my six years of schooling. Anxiety coursed through me as I weighed the idea, but my wife encouraged me to have the conversation, urging that a dialogue might provide new insights.

During that nerve-wracking call, Dr. Marx revealed that my major transgression was something I could hardly believe; I had simply omitted a single quotation mark in my citation. Reliving that moment even now stirs up feelings akin to PTSD from a decade ago; it's incredible how a small oversight can spiral into such turmoil. After that call, something shifted between us; we built a bond I never expected.

From that point forward, no bad grades followed, as I doubled my efforts in studying and engaged in meaningful communication with him. I passed the course with a respectable grade, yet I still felt a flicker of uncertainty about Dr. Marx. However, at the class's conclusion, he extended an invitation to all his students, encouraging us to stay in touch and offering ongoing coaching. After doing a little digging and reflecting on the connection we had forged through our phone conversations, I took the leap and scheduled my first appointment with him. Little did I know this would mark the beginning of an eight-year journey that would shape my life in profound ways.

In that time, our conversations transformed into deep discussions about faith, purpose, and the guiding presence of the Holy Spirit. We talked monthly on Thursday evenings, a time I cherished immensely. Each meeting lacked a formal agenda, but Michael had a quiet goal of nurturing my growth. His probing questions were unlike anything I had ever experienced—thought-provoking and deeply introspective. During one of our exchanges, he candidly told me, "Steve, you're not listening!" Those words struck me to my core, forcing me to confront my spiritual apathy.

What followed ignited a spark in my spiritual journey. Our conversations evolved into me sharing how the Holy Spirit was influencing my life. Although our phone calls became less frequent over the years, the bond we formed remained steadfast. Michael shared his own life experiences, weaving tales of his churches and practices, subtly enriching my understanding and fostering my faith. He became my prayer partner and my confidant, illuminating my path in ways I had never anticipated.

In my life, only a handful of men have earned a place on my pedestal, and Michael is undeniably one of them. I am forever grateful that God orchestrated our meeting and that he chose to pour his wisdom into my life. Michael offered me a much-needed aerial view of my path, enabling me to embark on a journey that aligned with God's intentions for me. It is my heartfelt pledge to Michael that I will continue to walk this path until the day we reunite.

> *Dave:* Michael was a significant part of my transition from vocational ministry to coaching in this latter third of my life. I recall chatting with him following one of our Coaching Ethics class sessions. In spite of being a little intimidated since he was my instructor, I quickly felt the warmth of his love for God and the coaching "ministry" God called him to. His presence and wisdom at each of our meetings were so impactful to me. And... who can forget your coaching book recommendations... particularly *The Little Engine That Could*! You, indeed, are a masterpiece created by the Master.

Steamboat Springs, Colorado

After training for two winters at the dog yard in Alaska, we moved the whole kit and caboodle to the Steamboat Springs area of Colorado in May 2015. We had a U-Haul pulling our car on a trailer and a dog truck holding 12 dogs. It took eight solid days to drive from Fairbanks to Colorado.

We rented a barn for a year from a woman who was the owner of a "growing" property. "Growing" in Colorado means you produce marijuana. Harvesting took place every 68 days and she would need people to trim the plants because harvestable marijuana grows in buds. Her harvesters would trim off the crystals and process them into a usable, smokable, or invertible product. For example, the crystals could be melted down and put into an oil or a gum product like a gummy bear. So, every 68 days, usually Joy, I, or my brother Fred would help the landowner with her harvest. We had some great conversations sitting around the table trimming marijuana. When you have it in your hands, on your clothes, and in your hair, you realize it's everywhere. After a long day of harvesting, I would walk down to our barn, remove all my clothes in front of the front door, and take a shower. Only then would I return to gather my clothes and toss them in the washer. They smelled incredibly bad!

Sharing

> *Kate:* Michael and I have shared a wonderful relationship through music dating back to the time of the COVID-19 pandemic when the world was shut up in darkness. We delighted in discovering and sending each other online links to the various recordings in creative renditions and in multiple languages from all over the world of "The Blessing." As much as my heart is saddened today by Michael's struggle and pain, my heart was always uplifted when I saw an email from Michael. I do not doubt that he has impacted others in similar ways through music and his extensive gifts and talents. I pray that we have all learned from his generous and caring soul.

I love to share. When I experience something meaningful, special, inspiring, happy, or even a meal, I want to share it. Maybe it's a movie. Or maybe it's a simple experience, but it makes me happy. I think it should be shared with other people. I'm constantly recommending movies, and especially books, to people. Hey, I was reading this book, and I really like it. Sometimes, I'll buy it and send it to them, but more times than not, I'll loan it, and the books usually come back. Very, very seldom have I ever loaned out a book that has not come back.

I also love telling people about our dogs and Joy's dog sledding business. It's the most fun you can ever have. I'd love to give away dog sledding tours all day long. This is Joy's business so I can't just give away her business for free. I find it so fun and inspiring.

Snow skiing is just as exhilarating. I love to teach people how to ski because I find it to be so fun. For me, it's a way of spreading joy and helping people have a higher level of life experience.

I keep what I call homeless kits in the car to give away to needy people on the street. These Ziploc bags are filled with a variety of items a homeless person might appreciate, such as a can of beans, a can of tuna fish, or maybe a little lunch pack of peaches. I would always include a gospel put together by an organization called PlusNothing.com. If you go to their website, they'll send you very nice versions of the gospels in chronological order for free, and they'll never bother you about donations. They arrive via FedEx within a couple of days. It's a top-shelf organization. Their aspiration is to give away 10 million gospels.

> **Kimberley:** Michael not only touched my life in a beautiful way with a heart, always ready to give and did his best to help others, but he was always encouraging others to do the same. The care packages made for the homeless were one of his ministries. As God provides, I plan on making care packages and giving them out.

There is no substitute for the joy giving generates. So much better than receiving. I love to share the love of something and potentially transfer it to another person, and possibly they will be an enthusiastic dog sledder, skier, or short story writer for the rest of their lives. For sharing is not only giving, but also inspiring for me as the giver. It makes me happy that something that I had was worth sharing. The enjoyment and appreciation that the receiver experiences inspire me to give more. The receiver is inspired to share more with others. When they reflect on their day, they can say, "Hey, I was able to share something with someone." Then they will also have a good feeling about themselves. I will keep doing that. We'll teach it to the children. And it will just keep moving forward.

It is so rewarding to know that what we have shared has made a difference in somebody's life. To touch them or help them move forward. Sharing is very cyclical.

Lisa Marx: Fred and I had the opportunity to live near Joy and Michael and their sled dogs in Colorado. One day, I wandered up to their house and was overcome by the rich aroma of freshly brewed coffee from Michael's Nespresso machine. Consistent with Michael's generous nature, he offered me a cup, and it was the best coffee I ever had. He coupled it with an engaging conversation rich in humor and knowledge. This became a routine in which I would visit, we'd talk, and then care for the sled dogs in the dog yard.

I found it incredible to participate in Michael's online celebration of life after his passing. His life was much larger than I had ever realized, and it impacted many more people than I could have imagined. Yet, I still remember Michael as the person with whom I shared countless coffees and conversations.

Pagosa Springs, Colorado

Written by Joy: Our move from the Steamboat Springs to Pagosa Springs in 2019 was truly miraculous in hindsight. Until that point in time, God had always guided us to the right place to live quickly and easily. However, when we started looking for a new rental property, nothing worked. During our nine-month-long search, one signed contract was rescinded; our next option burned to the ground before we could move in. Our last possibility had rattlesnakes. It was a very stressful time. Michael finally sent a text message to all his colleagues around the world asking for prayer. As a result, one person took the request to her prayer group. A man in the group contacted his friend in Texas who subsequently telephoned us with the offer of a great rental house for us and our dogs located in the national forest near Pagosa Springs. Upon researching the location, I discovered that the previous dog sledding operation had just closed. What a spiritual confirmation! So, we moved us, our dogs and my business to this new location in Colorado. We are continually grateful for God's guidance and miraculous provision.

Pagosa Living

Our local magazine is called *Pagosa Living*. I enjoy learning about events and activities but am particularly interested in the magazine introducing families and couples. The following two paragraphs represent what I submitted to the magazine.

We are Michael and Joy Marx, and we are known for the four D's. The first D is for dogs. Joy runs and operates Mountain Paws Dog Sledding in Pagosa Springs, Colorado. Our 20 Alaskan Huskies gleefully pull guests down a scenic trail for six-mile tours in the winter on snow, and they pull carts on wheels during the summer.

The second D represents our having lived in Deutschland (Germany) for 23 years of our adult lives. The third D is for dedication to each other, and the fourth D indicates devotion to one another and to God. We have been married for 40 years and tribute to this longevity is our devotion to each other.

> *Angie:* Michael, you have fought quite a fight! You not only have Joy by your side, but you also shine such joy from your heart. Getting to know you during our time doing the worship at Open Door Church, I always told you, "God Bless the sound guy!" The biggest job of the sound technician is to make the worship team sound good. What an inspiration you are. I applaud your great faith throughout your journey. Thanks for blessing us in Pagosa Springs.

Two Favorite Hacks

My first hack is ripening avocados. All of us in my household are very fond of avocados. The taste and the nutrition are very appealing to us. The problem with avocados is that they're expensive and rarely have the correct ripeness. If you want to buy them at the correct ripeness, they're usually very expensive.

We've discovered a way to get around all that. You can buy avocados in each stage of ripeness, even if they are as hard as a rock, which is usually less expensive. Put the avocados in a brown paper bag along with a piece of fruit such as a tangerine or apple. Close the bag tightly. Fruit gives off methane gas as it decomposes. In three to five days, the avocado is perfectly ripe.

The next simple yet effective hack has worked well for us over the years. I use mattress heaters and a heating blanket for my recliner. I prefer to heat the bed or chair rather than the entire room as it's more efficient. Plus, I can preset the mattress pad heater so that when I get into bed, it's already warm. Honestly, who cares if the air temperature is perfect?

With dual controls, Joy can adjust her heat preference independently. We switched to heated mattress pads about 20 years ago, and I've been satisfied ever since. We each get to enjoy our ideal temperature without having to fight over blankets or worry about adjusting the room's air temperature.

Oxygen

I'll never forget Halloween day, October 31, 2020. While I was in the dog yard scooping poop, I let the 17 dogs loose for a free run. No chains, no leashes, when suddenly I collapsed unconscious. Afterward, to my great surprise, I was able to corral the 17 dogs back to their houses.

This took place on a Saturday while Joy was visiting Milton and our grandson in Florida. She didn't return home until Monday evening. In her absence, I managed to get back inside the house and lay low until she arrived. Due to COVID restrictions, she took me to an urgent care facility instead of a hospital. While sitting in our car in the parking lot, I was diagnosed with pneumonia. Until that point, I didn't realize there were different types of pneumonia. Clinical pneumonia is what many people get when they are hospitalized, but I was diagnosed with wild pneumonia. I was sent home with antibiotics.

That night, I went to bed, but I had absolutely no energy. I couldn't even feed myself; I felt completely powerless. The worst part was that I was chilled to the bone and could not get warm. Despite taking antibiotics, I continued to struggle with my body temperature. Subsequently, the eventual solution was interesting and surprising. In the process of trying everything we knew to warm my body, we were given an oxygen condenser. As its name implies, the machine takes the ambient air and pushes it through a filter sending it through a tube and into my nose. The chills went away almost immediately. I usually use this oxygen condenser at night. My purpose for including this story is to inform you that oxygen is a remedy for the chills. I hope this makes a difference.

> *Joy:* The oxygen also helped with Michael's sleep apnea and consequently significantly decreased the snoring.

Call Me Michael (or Doctor)

Throughout my childhood and young adulthood, people called me Mike. To me, it sounded like a child's name. It wasn't until I was a youth pastor in 1991 that I claimed Michael as my only name.

My best friend was Ricky Smith, and when he turned 30, he declared that he wanted everyone to call him Rick. I thought, yes, it's an adult name. That's a good idea.

Yesterday, someone called me Mark. Since my name is Michael Marx, it's a common mistake. But I don't consider it to be very friendly when somebody calls me Mike or Mark. When the lady called me Mark, her husband corrected her and said, "His name is Michael," to which I agreed, "Yes, please call me Michael." Even after that, she asked, "Well, is it okay if I call you Mike?" And I said, "Absolutely not." I don't like it when someone takes liberties with a person's name. In my opinion, we should respect the right of a person to be identified according to their preference. In my classrooms even when I had 20 or even 30 students, I addressed each student by their chosen name with the pronunciation they wanted. When you're teaching people from other countries and other languages, names can get a little challenging. Regardless, I was (and still am) very conscientious with the pronunciation of a person's name.

These days, only academic and ski students call me Dr. Marx. In addition to academics, I'm a TSI, level one professional ski instructor. At Wolf Creek ski area near our home in Pagosa Springs, Colorado, they don't know me as Michael Marx; they refer to me as "Doctor." One of the supervisors in the ski school thought it was cool that he had a doctor of adult education on his professional ski instructor line-up. Ski instructors are more likely than not to be former athletes. We all call each other by our first names. However, this ski school decided that it would be cool to call me Doctor because they want the customers to know that we're not just a bunch of wild athletes.

Having a formal education on how adults learn has made a difference in how I teach. For example, I specialize in fear factors. Many people are very scared of skiing. I tell them that their fear is my specialty. I particularly enjoy adaptive ski instruction, such as teaching someone with PTSD, Down syndrome, MS, or fibromyalgia. I don't just work with the body as much as I do also with the brain.

> *Jeff:* Michael - A smart, friendly, decent person who honestly wants to help others. A treasured friend. I cherish the time we spent together. Mostly traveling to and from the ski hill. You were a fabulous, innovative ski instructor. So many accomplishments, hobbies, and interests, so much talent, caring, and passion are how I will always remember you.

> *Amanda:* (blind) Michael, knowing you has been the privilege of my life! My thoughts turn to the things we didn't get to do together this side of eternity: learning to ski, going dog sledding together... I promise to learn to ski, my friend, and I will love every minute because I know you will be there with me.

My Favorite Ski Lesson

It was spring break, March 2020, a blizzard condition day and not a nice day for ski lessons. But ironically, when people arrive for ski lessons, they are not very bothered by blizzards.

On this day, I heard a ruckus going on in one of the restrooms; yelling and screaming filled the building. Since I'm one of only a handful of licensed adaptive instructors, people trained in specialized training methodologies, the supervisor assigned the job to me.

I gulped as we unlocked the restroom. Standing there was a young man with a helmet, one ski glove, goggles, and one ski boot. I looked at him, and it took only seconds to determine that he was about 13 years old and high on the Down syndrome spectrum. "Hi.

My name is Michael. I'll be looking after you today." William returned the look with a smile that only people with Down syndrome can master.

Multiple cups of hot chocolate calmed him. Once we got his boots and skis on, I accompanied William onto the bunny slope for the usual beginners' shuffle, shuffle, shuffle, shuffle. Into the snow we went, and he was not very happy. Individuals high on the Down syndrome spectrum get frustrated very easily.

William started yelling loudly at me and the other adaptive instructors. Everyone on the bunny slope could hear him screaming at the top of his lungs. While the screaming itself isn't a problem, it can discourage other beginner skiers when someone sounds as if they're being murdered. It created a tense atmosphere on the bunny slope that March day. William wailed that he wanted his daddy and insisted that he wouldn't do anything without him. In my opinion, he wanted his dad there to see him ski, help him, and give him praise.

When his dad finally arrived, we were all sitting on the patio, sipping even more cups of hot chocolate. Though William had his skis on, he hadn't yet tried skiing. He looked at me point-blank and said, "I want a boat." I replied, "You want a what?!" He repeated, "I want a boat." I responded, "William, we're at 10,000 feet in the middle of the mountains. There are no boats here." He insisted, "I want a boat." I looked at his dad and mom, and they shrugged their shoulders.

Then what to my wondering eyes should appear, but a boat! Technically, it was a toboggan-shaped cargo sled used to haul ski poles from one rental shop to another. I lifted a praise, "Thank you, Lord Jesus. You provided us with a boat."

William, still ranting and making quite a spectacle of himself, was causing quite a ruckus near the top of the bunny slope. His dad and I removed all the ski poles from the sled, dragged it to the top of the bunny slope, and placed William in the cargo sled. We then started pulling him down toward the bottom of the bunny slope lift.

In the sweet way that only Down's people can do, he threw up his arms in his superhero position. "Show me your superpower!" With his arms over his head and at the top of his lungs, he then yelled, "I am the hammer. I am the hammer!" Williams's mom clarified, "That is what he says when he gets excited about his superpower."

Once we arrived at the bottom of the lift, I asked everybody to step aside; William went first. All the people at the bottom of the lift willingly stepped aside while William moved to the conveyor belt-style lift. I positioned myself on the conveyor belt so that William wouldn't slide off. Then I said, "Okay, everybody, give it up for William!" and everybody cheered for this disruptive 13-year-old who had never skied before. More than 100 people were screaming William, William, William! What a validating experience for him.

With his dad's help, we got William to the top of the conveyor belt lift and onto the snow. William independently slid down the bunny slope in his "boat." Everybody was cheering, hooting, and hollering as though he were Rocky Balboa on the Philadelphia Art Museum steps. William was cheering for himself. His mom was crying. His dad was videotaping all of it. The other skiers continued to cheer. Even I was crying as I followed him down the bunny slope. This was the coolest thing I'd ever done on skis. At the end of the day, William and I lay down in the snow and made snow angels.

A truly memorable moment, enhanced by a steaming cup of velvety hot cocoa. How often in your life can you pinpoint a specific incident or event where you genuinely impacted someone else's life for the better?

Fast forward two years, I spotted William's dad approaching me on the ski slopes. With excitement in his eyes, he shared the video from that unforgettable day. As we watched, I could see the joy on William's face. William still animatedly talks about his beloved boat, a testament to the lasting impression we made together.

Alphabet Soup

> *Joy:* Michael did not have the time nor the energy to cover all the topics that were dear to his heart: PCCI, CCNI, ICF, IRB, SUN, WCCWN, and CSA. With the help of his friends, I would like to make sense of the jumble of these letters.

Professional Christian Coaching Institute

Per their website, PCCI is "the world leader in virtual life and leadership coach training, providing education for those transitioning into the explosive new field of professional Christian coaching." After teaching some coaching courses for PCCI, Michael saw a need for a book on ethics. He undertook the project and wrote a very interesting book on a potentially uninteresting

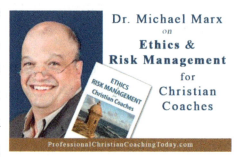

Dr. Michael Marx *on* **Ethics & Risk Management** for Christian Coaches

ProfessionalChristianCoachingToday.com

topic, which has since been used as the foundation in one of PCCI's required courses on ethics.

> *Christopher McCluskey:* At long last, an integration of our Christian worldview and morality with the standards and code of ethics of the International Coach Federation. Dr. Marx has blessed the Christian coaching community with a much-needed resource to elevate our professional standards of practice.

> **Phillip Janzen:** This is a thought-provoking, extremely useful desktop guide to those tough ethical situations one hopes never to face as a coach.

A podcast describing his book, morality, legality, and ethics: https://professionalchristiancoaching.com/051-dr-michael-marx-ethics-risk-management-christian-coaches/

> **Dale:** Michael, I recall that we first met in the PCCI Ethics Class. I confess that had it not been a required class, I probably would have skipped it as I thought I knew "all there was to know" about ethics. I quickly discovered I was wrong, and it became my favorite class of my PCCI education.

Michael's teaching for PCCI led him to **Convene**, for which Michael started the first online group. As described on their website, "Convene is a trusted community of Christian business leaders who meet monthly in peer-advisory teams across the world. Together, Convene members process opportunities and challenges, share priceless information from personal experience with each other, and grow in their faith through Christian executive learning content."

> **Harris:** Michael, I'm so grateful that God saw fit to cross our paths just a few years ago through Convene and PCCI. Because of you and your pouring into my life, I'm a better chair, coach, facilitator, and person. So thank you!

> **Lisa:** Thank you Michael for introducing me to Convene and helping create our wonderful team. I learned how to bring God's light into the workplace. You helped me develop into a leader. You also set so many amazing examples of how to live life, go with the flow and bless people through everyday work be it a ski instructor, coach or just driving down the street. Thank you for being the light our team needed.

Christian Coaches Network International

As a past president of CCNI, Michael's words can still be found on their website: "Since 2014, I have been involved with the 'forming, storming, norming' of the Christian Coaches Network International. My job was to lead the transition from an LLC to a 501(c)3. Numerous leaders in the Christian coaching industry have been very helpful in making CCNI the go-to place for all things relating to Christian coaching."

Upon learning of Michael's passing, CCNI wrote to their members.

> **CCNI:** Michael served multiple times as President of CCNI and was the driving force in making CCNI an international organization. He served as a teacher, mentor, and friend to many. His wisdom and insights were often just what was needed when decisions needed to be made, or challenges needed to be addressed. He presented many incredible coaching insights over the years with his intelligence, humor, and wisdom.
>
> If you scroll through the CCNI blog page and search his name you will find several articles written by Michael. He

also authored the most effective book on Christian Coaching Ethics... a foundation used by many to this day. He was a strong ethics leader for Christian coaching all around the world. One such post is *Ethics 101 - Taking the Holy Spirit Off Mute.*

On behalf of the entire CCNI board, **"Thank you, Michael.** Your love and dedication to God, to CCNI, and Christian coaching set a model for the future of Christian coaching. We love you with great love as our brother in Christ, mentor, and advocate for Christian coaching around the world."

International Coaching Federation (ICF) & Internal Review Board (IRB)

Per Wikipedia, ICF "is a non-profit organization dedicated to professional coaching. ICF is an accrediting and credentialing body for both training programs and coaches." ICF has more than 50,000 members in over 150 countries. Michael was very involved in many aspects of ICF.

Jürgen Bache describes his work with Michael for ICF:

Our collaboration began in 2011 when Michael stepped into the pivotal role of ICF sub-chapter host in Hanover within the framework of ICF Germany. With remarkable dedication and a strategic vision, he meticulously built up the sub-chapter from the ground up. Michael took on the responsibility of organizing a variety of impactful ICF events, fostering professional exchange around contemporary coaching topics. These gatherings featured a rich tapestry of lectures, workshops, and keynote speeches, often infused with engaging discussions and interactive elements to enhance the learning experience.

I had the privilege of witnessing Michael's expertise in the field of ethics flourish during his tenure as the leader of the Ethics Community of Practice from 2014 to 2019. Additionally, he pioneered the Ethics Watercooler discussion rounds, drawing participants from around the globe since 2014. Through these initiatives, he fostered a collaborative environment where a diverse group of coaches could engage in deep reflections about their practices and ethical dilemmas, significantly enriching their professional development.

His significant contributions as a co-author for the 2019 revision of the Code of Ethics (CoE) have had a lasting impact on the foundational ethical principles guiding ICF professionals. During the process of developing the ICF Ethics Interpretive Statements (EIS), which evolved into ICE—Insights and Considerations for Ethics—it consistently became evident that Michael's reflections transcended the surface-level inquiry often encountered. His ability to delve into the complexities of potential conflict situations allowed for thorough consideration, description, and even preemptive resolutions for challenges that ICF professionals might face.

Within the coaching community and beyond, Michael earned recognition as an outstanding expert on issues pertaining to coaching practice and ethics. His profound influence enhanced the quality of coaching delivered by ICF professionals committed to the Code of Ethics, further solidifying the critical role of coaching in society at large.

Since 2016, Michael has been an invaluable volunteer on the ICF's Independent Review Board (IRB), an independent ethics committee serving as an arbitration board. Until his recent illness, he shaped the work of this essential group with his extensive knowledge, a wealth of experience, and, notably, his characteristic humor that lightened even the most serious discussions.

Michael's absence is deeply felt—not only by his friends but by a global community of professional coaches who have benefited immensely from his insights and contributions.

Todd: Michael's impact will be felt within ICF and the coaching profession for many years to come. His love of ethics has made the entire profession better, and his humor, compassion, and wisdom have made all of us better.

Laura: Michael, you were one of the first people to welcome me to the IRB and show me what our work is all about. I was immediately struck by your deep caring, respect, and commitment in equal parts for every person you interact with, as well as the ethical work we do. I love your humor, your heart, your dedication, and your willingness to say what needs to be said. You have inspired me in so many ways and continue to do so.

Katherine: Michael, we worked together for many years on the IRB and I always enjoyed our conversations. To me, you have always been so focused on your service, committed to ethics, passionate about, and eager to share your perspective and knowledge.

Philip: Michael, thank you for being a shining light in the ICF ethics community. You created a safe space to share, explore, dissect, and push back on the code. I will always be thankful for "Rule 29". (Don't be stupid!) It is the most insightful rule, even if it's not official. Your absence from the coaching conversation has been felt deeply. I'm sure your voice will continue in my head when I have discussions about ethics.

Annie: Michael, When I felt called to participate in the ICF Community of Ethics, I was so drawn to your open, direct, gentle style. I was quite an active participant for a while merely because you created such a safe space.

Success Unlimited Network (SUN)

Per the website: "SUN is a global network of Coaches, Coach Educators, Coach Mentors, Coach Supervisors and coaching leaders who inspire purposeful being for the evolution of humanity."

Teri-E Belf, SUN Founder & Executive Director:

> Interesting that this one memory keeps popping up because I have soooo many memories of knowing Michael from the past 10 years. Passion for Ethics bonded us.
>
> For this memory, we were in person at a SUN coaching retreat in 2022 in Eilat, Israel. I observed and heard Michael's joy at experiencing something new. He loved the people, the environment, the different religions, the food, everything. He even loved swimming and joined our Coordinator for VERY early morning swims in the cold Red Sea.
>
> Professional roles cast aside, we were just 2 friends exploring the wonder of a new experience in the world. It was the last day, and our group went to the city to gather souvenirs to take home. We ended up walking together. I think Michael came with me because walking alone at night is not the safest thing to do in a foreign city. He was my watchdog in unspoken words. He is a walking-talking, do-the-right-thing kind of guy. He even contributed our most infamous and discussed standard #28 in our coaching

Code of Ethics: *I am aware of my and my clients' impact on society. I adhere to the philosophy of "doing good" versus "avoiding bad."* This is Michael, always doing good in service on all levels.

I had a shopping mission to find a 'shoehorn' to fulfill my Grandson's request. Michael's mission was just to be who he was and enjoy the experience internally and externally with calmness, curiosity, gusto, loving connections, and presence. We spoke to many people along the way, learning more about 'who' they were. We scoured the entire town for 1.5 hours, talking about superficial things and deep, profound spiritual philosophies while going into every shop in search of a shoehorn. The only break was when Michael sat on a bench and made a phone call. I am sure it was to Joy.

Suddenly, I realized that we had no more time. However, there was one last shoe store to explore. When the clerk bent down to look and produced an unopened shoehorn package, I screamed. Michael charged in when he heard me scream. We laughed so hard, and I realized how safe I felt when I was with him.

Afterward, at the closing ceremony, Michael gave me a gift from one of our craft activities. Michael had made a simple colorful airplane out of popsicle sticks. I have it poised, landing on my favorite plant. I treasure it and him for all the years of sharing and creating memories.

Wolf Creek Christian Writer's Network

WCCWN is a local group of aspiring and published writers.

Joyce: Michael, I appreciate our shared professional background in teaching ESL. (English as a Second Language) I suspect we are both "weird" in that we enjoy grammar and are more watchful in that regard in our writing and teaching. To me, your short grammar quizzes in the writers' group added some "spice" to our learning.

Faith: At WCCWN, you helped develop me as an upcoming writer with critique and criticism. Thank you for sharing your heart with me at church and expressing your admiration for watching me perform sign language in worship. You encourage me to keep pursuing this passion I have for Jesus.

Kimberley: Michael, when I first met you in the writer's group, I watched as you led the group through technology where so many of us had no clue. You always did your best with such great patience to make sure our meetings ran smoothly. (Not always an easy task) Then, sitting in a critique group listening to your wisdom and trying to learn from your encouragement, as well as listening to your unique and heart-touching "stories from the heart," was a treat and a true blessing!

Coaching Suicide Awareness (CSA)

Michael founded and was president of CSA, whose stated mission is to "provide networking and resources for suicide readiness training for professionals, including coaches who are dedicated to saving lives and bringing hope to those contemplating or affected by suicide." Michael expresses this passion himself in the Caring Bridge post found at the end of this book.

> **Doreen:** Coaching Suicide Awareness - Michael, your passion to build an education and coach awareness program to empower us speaks to your advocacy for professional coaching. What a beautiful legacy you have built in the many lives you have touched and mentored. Thank you for believing in me as a coach, speaker, and panelist.

The Don Quixote Group

aka The Four Best Friends

Kees: How does a group of men working together on a philosophical project become a group of close friends? Quite simply, in the course of their work, they realize that they share the same values, that they see the world with very alert and critical eyes, and that they appreciate and exchange ideas. It was a happy coincidence that all four of them are also passionate coaches.

Besides our original leader and best friend, American Michael, there are three others to mention firstly Juergen, a broad-minded, people-oriented, open-skeptic German, then Gürkan, a broadly understanding, upright, people-person Turk, and finally Kees, a creative, free-thinking, humanist Dutchman.

The first topics at the monthly meetings between the four of them revolved around improvements in the coaching world and the common denominator ICF. The name Don Quixote, which the group gave itself, spoke for itself. There were and are many windmills to be tilted at. Some changes in the ethical world of coaching could also be initiated through the different honorary positions of the four.

A long weekend together in Amsterdam showed even more clearly how much power there was in this group. Thanks to Kees' local knowledge of where you can dine fantastically, that enjoyment is not neglected despite all the work.

The renaming of the group to four best friends was obvious because the focus was not on joint resistance to grievances but on unity and creativity.

After Michael's illness, it was particularly important to accompany him, to stand by his side even from thousands of kilometers away.

We miss our best friend, Michael, dearly. And how grateful we are to have had such a deep friendship with him.

Michael: The four of us have had some success in effecting change in international ethics standards. For example, we changed the International Coaching Federation (ICF) Code of Ethics. Number nine now states that a client can cancel the coaching conversation at any time for any reason, no questions asked. This change is a direct result of the four of us getting together to formulate new verbiage, which we subsequently turned over to the ICF organization and which ultimately became

part of the new code. Not only are we best friends, but we have achieved results such as this example by discussing key issues for over 10 years.

They are amazing best friends. We just spoke this morning (2/20/24), and they were expressing their concern and love for me as they have for the past six months since I was diagnosed with brain cancer. It was very, very touching.

Final Musings

Mentoring

My good friend, Walt Hastings, says that coaching is dragging potential/thoughts out from people; mentoring is putting it into them. Since my dissertation research was on coaching and mentoring relationships, I've done a lot of academic research on both ways of working with people. I think mentoring is more fun because in a mentoring relationship, the mentee wants you to tell stories, and I'm a good storyteller.

I have enjoyed many mentor-mentee relationships over these past years. I enjoy how the mentee is innately curious about how I handle things in my life successfully and unsuccessfully. For example, this afternoon I have a call scheduled. We talk about once a month anywhere from 20 minutes to 2 hours per session, and we've been doing this for 10 years. We talk about God, relationships, religion, business, and economics.

I think the key to good mentoring is trust, which enables a person to speak one's mind without fear of sounding stupid or being criticized. A trusting relationship is the key to good mentoring. Mentoring allows me to pour ideas into somebody in such a way that they respond with curiosity and continue to ask questions. Their interest is very high regarding how I have handled business situations, personal relationships, and other such topics. These young men (primarily) are working out how to be husbands, fathers, bosses, or business owners.

Over the years in my role as coach, consultant, mentor, or whatever hat I am wearing, I've discovered a very valuable communication technique. The mentee expresses their reflections to me, and I reflect the information back to them.

One person said, "When I talk to you, I'm able to bring the last two months into a stream of consciousness. If I talk to Michael on a regular basis, my life makes more sense." I consider that to be a great honor.

> **Diane:** Michael has been my mentor coach for a number of years, and we've had deep conversations of faith during those sessions. Michael carries the Mind of Christ even if his brain is under attack. And that mind flourishes... I have seen it connected with the compassion he carries for others.

How I wish I had had a mentor when I was in my mid-30s! I could have been smarter if I had sought one out, but I didn't know how valuable it could be.

There is a very popular question about legacy in coaching. So, you're sitting on your porch, and you're 80 years old. And next to you is a basket where you've dropped written notes about the things that you regret. What is in that basket? As we do this exercise, the notes almost always say, "I should have spent more time building relationships and less time building my business." That's the universal answer.

This question was asked in senior living facilities in 1989 in Berlin, Germany. The people answering this question were those who had survived World War II. Thousands of Berliners were asked, "What do you regret?" Many answered that they should have taken more risks. That survey profoundly influenced me because I was in my late 20s when I learned this. I thought, "Oh, that's not going to happen to me when I'm 80 years old. I'm not going to say that I wished I had taken more risks, but probably going to say I wish I'd taken fewer risks." Ultimately, that survey shifted my mindset from being risk averse, to more risk loving.

For example, if I go into a restaurant, especially where I've never been to before, I will find the one thing on the menu that I am unfamiliar with and order it. My wife thinks that's silly because what if I don't like it? That's never happened. I'll pretty much eat anything. If I order it and pay for it, I'll eat it. And nowadays I think, "What's it going to do, kill me?" Big deal, right?

You can take risks with food; you can take risks by driving home a different way; you can take risks by going into a particular shop even if it looks dingy on the outside. We recently drove past a place called the Billy Goat Saloon. It was flanked with a big mural of a Billy goat on the front. I suggested to my wife that we should stop there and see what the Billy Goat Saloon offers. She just looked at me like I couldn't be serious. No, not serious, but curious. I can be very curious.

The Week that Rocked My World

The beginning of that momentous week in August 2023 started in March. I noticed that I was not running at full speed; I was fatigued. My spatial ability and depth perception were compromised. I could still drive at that point in time, but by April I had an underlying feeling that something was not right.

On August 12, 2023, a Saturday morning, I was driving to a men's prayer breakfast at church. Not only did I turn the wrong direction, but I also drove through a red light and got pulled over. The officer assessed me, and asked, "Are you alright?" I replied, "I don't know. I might be anemic." He said, "Well, you'd better get that checked out."

After a visit to the doctor with the required blood tests, nothing was revealed to prevent me from flying to Europe (Sunday, August 20, 2023.) Although this was a business trip to Slovakia, I had decided to first visit my cousins in Budapest, Hungary since they lived relatively close to my destination. Joy was still very concerned and reserved gate assistance at each of the airports. At the last minute, she also booked travel insurance, thank God!

Later I learned from the neurosurgeons that 30,000-foot altitudes and brain tumors don't go well together. The two together wreaked havoc in the air. Any slight symptoms I was previously exhibiting were greatly exacerbated.

Upon arriving in Budapest on Monday morning, I was met by my cousin Istvan and his lovely wife Anna. We took off through the countryside to visit Imre, Istvan's brother. I remember the drive to his house made me nauseous because curvy European country roads are ubiquitous.

We had lunch at Imre's house, featuring bean soup, a staple served to the Hungarian Marx kids every day after school. The next stop was Monica's house. She was married to Istvan Bozoky, and together they owned and operated the finest vineyard in Hungary producing exquisite Riesling wines. A wine museum is part of the property with a vaulted wine cellar. Located in Mori, Hungary, this property pays homage to the traditional heritage of fine wine makers. Monica decided the best thing for an upset stomach was a couple of glasses of Riesling wine. Great idea. She was confident it was the elixir for all ailments. In the evening, I returned to Istvan's home.

I became very alarmed about my own ability to perform basic functions when trying to get from my bed to the toilet. When I slipped and fell in the bathroom, I also became concerned about my own safety.

On Tuesday I took the train from Budapest to Bratislava, Slovakia, and was met at the train station by my teaching partner, Marian Kubes. We went to his house for the evening where I once again slipped and fell in his bathroom. Marian had already observed that I wasn't acting like my former self. The next day he became increasingly alarmed and called an ambulance. The lights and sirens only served to emphasize how my world had turned upside down. I was taken to the neurology ward of the Slovakian Technical University Hospital.

Marian also canceled the teaching seminar that we had planned for the rest of that week. He said he would teach it if I had to stay in the hospital. He was fully qualified to teach it. I was a little disappointed because I liked teaching the class which was called Advanced Life Coaching. It's a great group of students. They are very curious, very intelligent. Half are nuns and the other half are priests. Even though I was disappointed, I saw the wisdom in Marian teaching the class while I rested in the ICU of the hospital's neurology ward.

On Thursday the 24th of August, I was diagnosed with two brain tumors. The first tumor was about the size of a tangerine, and it sat in the middle of my skull. Flying back to the States was out of the question as it would have been life-threatening according to the doctors. The smaller tumor was located on the occipital lobe and was inoperable due to its location. I texted Joy telling her that I was in the hospital with a diagnosed brain tumor, which required surgery. She arranged to leave on the same day but arrived from the United States two days later due to a missed connection. She immediately took charge.

Brain surgery was scheduled for September 14. Unfortunately, it had to be rescheduled because I experienced a sudden excruciating pain in my abdomen the night before the operation. Due to a tear in the bowel, I had emergency abdominal surgery at midnight. Consequently, the brain surgery had to be postponed until I could adequately recover from the abdominal surgery.

> *Joy:* In preparation for the surgery, the neurosurgeon described how they planned to cut out a piece of the cranium. He looked at Michael and said, "Don't worry! I'll glue it back on."

Finally on September 20, the large tumor was removed. Everybody who looked at the resection, CT scan or MRI, said it was a very well-executed surgery. This is very important because this was a glioblastoma multiforme (GBM) tumor whose cells can very quickly, in fewer than 11 days, mutate into a new GBM tumor the size of a golf ball and be just as deadly. In the world of oncology, the GBM is known as 'the Terminator' because it is 100% deadly and 100% nasty.

The primary goal over the next two weeks became getting me back to the United States. I needed to get back home to an environment that was more conducive to my lifestyle and in a language that we could speak and understand. Given Joy's expertise as a former travel agent and being the great organizer that she is, she got it all worked out. We flew home on October 5.

With Kat's assistance and Joy's oversight, I am now part of the Medicaid system. It was a lot of work getting all the paperwork for that kind of thing completed. Since arriving back in the United States, I have been in palliative care which focuses on extending the quantity and quality of life.

I'm so glad that Joy is the quarterback on my team. She is doing an amazing job extending my life primarily through diet. We are convinced with a lot of help from our friends that nutrition is the way to stay alive. Of course, this applies to anyone whether you have cancer or not. Our favorite source is a book by Dr. Joel Fuhrman called *Eat to Live.* I recommend that everybody read it. It emphasizes good nutrition through homemade plant-based foods, no sugar, no processed foods, just a healthy diet.

Since returning to the United States, I have been learning new ways to exercise, eat healthy foods, and live. I fatigue quickly. Loud noises rattle my brain. For example, going to church where everybody's in one big room talking, laughing and singing, well... that is just hard to handle.

Otherwise, I must say my quality of life is very high and I have my wife to fully thank for that. I also thank all of you reading this text since I know you have been praying for me. I have seen how many people have been keeping up with this journey through Caringbridge.org. I am overwhelmed by the amount of love and concern and prayers that have been posted. Thank you all so much!

> *Joy:* The story of Michael's journey through brain cancer starting in August 2023 and culminating in April 2024 is recorded in the Caring Bridge posts, which are included at the end of this book.

> *TJ:* Michael, I only met you once. I had the honor to simply be with you for a few hours late in December. (2023) I knew nothing about your life. We sat in your office together and you talked, reminisced about a life well-lived. Of course, you did not use those words, they are completely mine. I became more and more fascinated with the story of your life and work, of your and Joy's adventures together, of your absolute love for, and faith in your Lord and Savior. And then ... your more recent "story." A turn in life's events that rattled your and Joy's world. Shaken, but not broken, I have witnessed this in the both of you together. The suddenness of your illness is life-shattering for so many people. You have touched so many people in so many ways.

Praying Friends

As a Christian, it's been amazing to witness who has been praying for me through this brain cancer ordeal. This morning, one of them said to me, "Imagine my hand is on the lower part of your back and I'm praying that God reduces your headaches as you receive this chemotherapy." I thought, wow, this is amazing! An atheist is praying for my healing. It is because of love. It's just so amazing to have such close friends.

Conventional Christianity teaches us to evangelize and tell people about Jesus, so that they may be saved by accepting the Lord as their Savior. That's one of our religion's primary tenets, to inspire people to be Christians. To quote Timothy, "For God hath not given us the spirit of fear [timidity]; but of power, and of love, and of a sound mind." 2 Timothy 1:7 (KJV) This means that we have boldness to preach the gospel. When one of my friends says, "I'm praying for you," theologically speaking, he's entering the same space that Jesus is right now at the right hand of the Father. He has entered that same spiritual space to pray for me as I pray for him. How cool is that? And sometimes in evangelism, we make things so unbelievably complicated.

Yet, what it comes down to is relationship. Trust. I have been told, "I trust you more than anyone." If I tell my friend, "You can walk up to the throne of God and ask for prayer for yourself or for me or for anyone else, God will hear your prayers." My friend is going to believe me because he trusts and loves me. I just think we sometimes make it way too complicated. It's not about tips and tricks and theology and arguments and winning philosophies that will convince people that one way of believing is better than another. It's about relationships.

What will come out of the relationship years down the road? One day one of my friends may need spiritual intervention. At some point they might think about calling on that God of Michael's. They'll remember. In Daniel Chapter 3, we are introduced to King Nebuchadnezzar of Babylon who thought he was hot stuff. He declared that everybody should bow down and worship his golden image. He was just going to go ahead and be God. Well, that didn't work out so well. God said, I don't think so. In fact, for the next seven years, you're going to roam the earth like a cow, eating grass. And when Nebuchadnezzar finally came out of his stupor, he rescinded his proclamation and said, "Do not worship me.

Instead, worship the God that delivered Shadrach, Meshach, and Abednego from the burning furnace as well as Daniel from the lion's den. That's the real guy. That's the one you need to worship. Not some human fraud like me." So, the people and Nebuchadnezzar remembered the real God.

My prayer is that people looking back to 2024 remembering Michael Marx going through the burning fire will realize that Michael´s God is spiritually powerful and is the One they need to call on. They will enter that holy space at the right hand of the Father where Jesus is sitting and will call upon Jesus to answer their prayers.

In Psalms, we learn that everything we do ultimately influences other people in what they do. All of which should further the kingdom of God. In the book of Galatians, this is referred to as love, joy, peace, patience, gentleness, tenderness, goodness, and self-control. These are the fruits of the Spirit.

Heaven is going to be like that moment when my friend said, "Imagine my hand is on the small of your back and I'm praying that your pain will diminish." That feeling, the love and gratitude and belonging, and joy, is what we will experience in heaven. One person described it as elation. It's those moments of elation where you say, "Oh wow, that is so good. That is so cool. That is so warm. That is so tranquil. That is so loving." That is what heaven will feel like.

Imagine a moment of elation you experienced today. Now, multiply that feeling times by 24/7. That's what heaven will feel like... that moment of elation. I asked Joy this question yesterday, and she shared that day's moment of elation with me. She dragged a pallet out to her dog sledding trail, turned it sideways and created a snow bridge. There was a small creek crossing her trail, which had never frozen over. It had prevented her from running the dog sled teams in this area of the ranch. So, she took a pallet or two and took them out there, laid them sideways across the trail, and packed them down with snow. Consequently, she can run her tours almost normally through the whole ranch. She was pleased with herself and proud of herself and the results. That feeling multiplied by 24/7 is what heaven will be like.

I've been reading a lot on heaven and recommend Randy Alcorn's *Heaven* more than any other book I have read so far. *The Shack* by William P. Young is also highly recommended by myself and my brother Fred who said it was the most impactful book he had ever read.

Michael's Four Values

Joy: Michael often created acronyms to remember many different ideas and lists. To remember the values listed below, just think of RICE.

Here we go!

#1. R=Respect. Respect means that other people's values are as important or more important than yours, so when it's important to them, it becomes important to you.

For example, if somebody says it's important to me that you're on time, they are saying that punctuality is an important value to them. Point of fact, Germans feel very disrespected when you consistently don't show up on time.

#2. I=Integrity. If I say I am going to do something, I do it. It is important to me that I exhibit that value in what I do. Integrity is doing what is right, even when no one else is watching.

#3. C=Consideration. Consideration is a part of respect. For example, last Saturday we had sausages, and I pulled out the mustard. I kept it as far away from Joy as possible because she hates even the smell of it.

#4. E=Encouragement: Helping people move forward is encouragement.

> *Joy:* This seems to be a good place to share one of Michael's favorite quotes, which he wanted to share with everyone. It's from the book, *It's Not Easy Being Green* by Jim Henson, The Muppets and Friends.
>
> > If just one person believes in you
> > Deep enough and strong enough
> > Believes in you hard enough and long enough
> > Before you know it, someone else would think

"If he can do it, I can do it"

Making it two.

Two whole people who believe in you.

And maybe even you can believe in you too.

~Robin and the Muppet Gang

I recently Googled the quote and discovered that the Muppets had turned this quote into a song in tribute to Jim Henson's life. It brought tears to my eyes as the things the Muppets said about Jim Henson could easily be applied to Michael.

https://www.youtube.com/watch?v=SRSptCfn5WY

My Place in the Sun

Sunshine has turned out to be one of the most medicinal, helpful assets that I can hold onto during a day. In my case, the sun comes through my bedroom window and lands right on my pillow between 2 and 3:30 in the afternoon. This is the optimum time for me to take an afternoon nap. Conversely, it's also a very good time to get visitors, and a very good time to talk to my sister. So, there's a lot of competition for this timeslot. Nevertheless, I've noticed half an hour in the sun cures all ills; it erases the disorientation, and it takes away stomachaches. It eliminates a headache. It's medicinal on all fronts. I haven't researched the science, but it's commonly known that you need vitamin D directly from the sun every day.

As I talk to people and gather prayer requests from around the world, I hear that a lot of people have overactive immune systems which are causing swelling and fatigue. I am recommending to them that they sit more in the sun each day. The reports that I'm getting are very positive. We know that sunshine is a beckoning

call for people all over the world. We gravitate to beaches, lake shores, swimming pools, etc. Sunshine is a cure. I'm surprised at how much I enjoy just sitting in the sunshine.

Now I will go back to basking in the remaining 30 minutes of direct sunlight coming through my window.

Prayers

I am spending my final days praying for those I call or hear from. This calling had given the remainder of my life purpose. Prayer requests come from across the country ranging from hip replacements, repeat COVID, immigration dilemmas, spouses not talking to each other, and pain in many different forms and fashions, physical, mental, and spiritual. Often people need wisdom for business decisions. Sometimes I ask a person how I can pray for them, and they say, "That's a good question, Michael. I don't know." So, I suggest, "Well, this is what I'm going to do. I'm going to pray that your designated one (husband, daughter-in-law, whomever you want prayer for) becomes closer to God and that they have a deeper relationship with the Trinity God: the

Father, the Son, and the Holy Spirit. Most people respond well to that suggestion because it acknowledges that there is spiritual pain. Perhaps we just don't want to have separation or isolation from God. Consequently, I have noticed that most prayer requests fall into three basic categories: healing, quality of life and a loved one's relationship with the Triune God.

I encourage you to pray diligently. Recently I have done much of my praying in the middle of the night. Chemo and steroids often cause me to lie awake between midnight and six a.m. Instead of tossing and turning, I spend the time praying during what my mother used to call "the prayer hours." In her opinion, the only useful things that happen between three and six o'clock in the morning are intercessory prayers. I recently realized that many things my mother did during the last five years of her life, I'm doing now. She would spend hours each day on the phone, talking to people about their prayer requests, and then spend half the night praying for them. How interesting that this routine has recently become my lifestyle.

To stay organized, I tack sticky prayer notes on a wall map. I am reminded of the movie "The War Room" starring Priscilla Shirer, in which the character used her closet to pray without distraction. My current prayers are based on, inspired by, and guided by the Lord's Prayer: Our Father who art in heaven, hallowed be thy name. Thy kingdom come; thy will be done on earth as it is in heaven. Jesus taught us to start our prayers by glorifying God. You then tell God, "I know you can do this. And I'm so looking forward to heaven where I will not have a bad heart, where my children will be enjoying you in your fullness and in the hope of salvation, where we are all able to rest in heavenly peace throughout a very long eternity enjoying God. Lord, shower us with a little bit of that heaven on Earth." In Heaven I can live with peace, without the heart murmur, without the lack of money or other physical or tangible deficiency. I am grateful every day in which I can pray for other people while contemplating eternity, which for me is right around the corner.

Many years ago, I could never have imagined that I would pray for multiple hours each night. My mother did it regularly, and I looked upon that with wonder. Now, at 62 years old, I find prayer to be an anchor in my life. I am able to fill every day with meaningful activity, most of which is centered around praying for other people. Unanticipated!

When I am done, my spirit is at peace. That peace is a gift back from God because He's given us the spirit of peace. Experiencing the peace he has gifted us with is a form of worshiping Him. Our chief aim is to **glorify God and to enjoy him forever**.

One of my goals is to have a 65th birthday party to celebrate surviving cancer. It is one of the things that I am most looking forward to. But even more than a party, I'm looking forward to heaven and living in harmony, in fellowship and in eternal worship of the Father, the Son, and the Holy Spirit.

My mother used to say, "All is well" when asked how she was. This really meant, "It is well with my soul." I understand this peace and grace all too well now.

Joy: Michael chose this song to most represent his life. He wanted to share with others. "Only Jesus" by Casting Crowns
Casting Crowns - Only Jesus (Official Lyric Video)
And the verse is:

> I don't want to leave a legacy
> I don't care if they remember me
> Only Jesus
> I've only got one life to live
> I'll let every second point to Him
> Only Jesus

I'm going to take this opportunity to say something I've already said. Philippians 1:21 states, "For to me, living means living for Christ, and dying is even better." I'm walking through life right alongside Jesus. He is also where I'm going next. When I die, I get to walk alongside Christ in heaven, and celebrate God and eternity with God, which I am very much looking forward to. I have done a lot of research into heaven in the last couple of months. Probability theory says that I will not be alive by Christmas 2024. **All is Well!**

Sadistics

Sadistics = statistics: I define this as the study of absolute meanness and standard deviousness. As to the academics, I liked the results, not the process of generating the numbers. Statistics was the only graduate school class in which I did not excel.

In my situation, three dates repeatedly pop up as reliable statistical data for people with GBM (Glioblastoma Multiforme) tumors. This creates a couple of benchmarks in my life. The first statistic is a lifespan prediction of 15.25 months from the date of detection. Research in over 14,400 people with GBM tumors states that most are unlikely to still be alive after 15.25 months, which brings my life expectancy to Christmas 2024.

I can look at these so-called prognosis dates in two ways. One I will be dead, or two I will be alive; either alternative is fine with me. I look forward to next Christmas one way or another. In the meantime, I wake up every day, thinking, hey, I am still alive. I've got another day to glorify God and enjoy Him forever. On earth as it is in heaven. What can I do today to glorify God? What can I do until my time comes? There is a line from a popular Christian song: "On that day when my strength is failing, the end draws near, and my time has come. Still, my soul sings your praises unending, 10,000 years and then forevermore." (10,000 Reasons Bless the Lord) I think of the Westminster catechism answer to question number one. The chief aim of men is to glorify God and enjoy him forever. I can enjoy Him every day; I wake up and think,

"Thank you. I'm alive." So, 15.25 months? I'll take it. Let's go. Let's have another glorious day.

Benchmark #2 is 18.5 months from the date of diagnosis, which is approximately March 17, 2025, the date of our 41st wedding anniversary.

Benchmark #3 is a 5-year prognosis, which is rare. Few have survived a GBM tumor for more than five years. This disease is known in the oncology world as the "Terminator."

As its nickname implies, no known cure, 100% lethal. When I say such things to my friends, especially my Christian friends, some of them get mad at me. Like oh my god, that's a defeatist attitude, bro. Well, I'm not accepting this as my sentence. I'm not saying God has declared that I will be dead by Christmas this year. I understand why people recoil. Just because some rigorous, scientifically proven test has come up with a timeframe doesn't mean that I plan on leaving. It's my life and I intend to celebrate Christmas.

So, if I'm alive tomorrow, I get to help some more people get a perspective on heaven. Hallelujah. And if I am not alive tomorrow, then I will get my own perspective on heaven. **Hallelujah!!!**

Michael entered heaven on April 30, 2024.

Michael's friends and colleagues created this plaque describing the qualities and characteristics they saw in Michael. It was a very special gift.

Debbie: One question Michael liked to ask was, "What did you learn about yourself in that situation?" I used that question last week with my son, and we had a great conversation. That's a small example of how Michael used coaching questions to really engage all those he met. He was naturally curious and loved going deep with people. After Michael passed away, we had three Zoom "tributes" where people could share a memory or story. One person said, "I'm confused. I thought I was Michael's best friend," and everyone in the room laughed because we all felt close to Michael. I thought to myself, "How can one person impact such a wide variety of people from so many different backgrounds and cultures?" Michael impacted my life in so many ways. I am forever grateful for his friendship. What did I learn from his life and death? Be curious, take time for people, and enjoy the life you have been given.

The End

Caring Bridge

Introduction

This collection of posts on caringbridge.org starting with the diagnosis of Michael's brain tumor provides an intimate insight into Michael and Joy's lives, faith and passions. Primarily written by Joy, it is full of prayerful, serious and light-hearted musings.

Family, Friends & Prayer Warriors

August 27, 2023 - Joy

First of all, thank you so much for the outpouring of love, concern, prayers and good wishes that have come to us from around the world. It is so special and comforting to know that all of you are praying for us and for Michael's recovery.

Quick summary: For the second year in a row, Michael has traveled to Bratislava, Slovakia to conclude a coaching seminar in person, which he has been teaching online for the last 6 weeks. Prior to the trip, Michael showed signs of increasing exhaustion. He visited his local physician. Neither the exam nor his blood work gave us reason to cancel the trip. We both felt he was supposed to go.

 On Sunday the 20th, Michael left Colorado and traveled first to Hungary where he had been very much looking forward to visiting his cousins. On Wednesday the 23rd, he traveled to Bratislava by train. By the next day, his condition had deteriorated so much that he was transported to the hospital where tests revealed that he has a brain tumor, which requires surgery. Of course, I made immediate plans to join him and finally arrived yesterday (Saturday) afternoon. He had been in the ICU since arrival. I was able to help get him transferred to a regular hospital room. His physical and cognitive condition has improved probably due to his medications to reduce the swelling in his brain. Tomorrow (Monday) we have an appointment for an MRI, which will show the brain in much more detail.

As today is Sunday, I did not expect much activity, but God works in amazing and miraculous ways: One of Michael's seminar participants is a friend of Dr. S., a renowned oncologist and member of the World Health Organization. Even though Dr. S. travels around the world, he happened to be in Slovakia today before traveling on to Africa. After attending his church, Dr. S. gave me half an hour out of his schedule to discuss Michael's situation. He contacted another friend, a neurosurgeon who studied and worked in Germany for many years. This surgeon has recently returned to Slovakia to work in a brand new hospital, which just opened here in Bratislava a few months ago. Even though this neurosurgeon is currently on vacation, he and his team will be reviewing the results of Michael's MRI scan tomorrow to decide when to proceed with the surgery. I am simply overwhelmed by the miraculous way in which this group of professionals has shown interest in Michael.

Discouraging to Encouraging

August 29, 2023 - Joy

This day, which began with some discouragement, ultimately turned into encouragement. Battling the intense and continuous hiccups for the last 5 days has been very challenging emotionally and physically. These hiccups are being fired up by the tumor. Maybe it's the body's way of sounding the alarm. (OK! Message received. Now would someone please turn off the alarm?)

Yesterday's MRI revealed that the tumor was not immediately life-threatening, thereby not requiring immediate emergency surgery. Consequently, I had become concerned that we might have to wait a long time before surgery would be scheduled. Praise God: Dr. T., the neurosurgeon on vacation, called Michael's doctor (Dr. G.) while I was expressing my concerns to him. Dr. T. informed Michael's doctor that his team was trying to move around various patients to make space for Michael's surgery.

On the way to the hospital this morning, God gave me a message: Luke 1:74-75

God gave... "a promise to free us from the power of our enemies, (brain tumor) so that we could serve Him without fear in a way that is holy and right for as long as we live." I believe that this is also the desire of Michael's heart.

My Dad

August 30, 2023 - Kat

I woke up this morning to the news that my dad was getting moved back to the ICU wing in the hospital. My mom handed the phone over to my dad. In that moment my mind short circuited, I didn't quite know what to say, to cry, to suck it up, to be happy or depressed. Subconsciously, I opted for the here and now. Unable to stop the silent tears falling down my face, I asked him how he was doing. He was slow to respond. "Don't be discouraged," I told myself. He conveyed that he was doing alright.

My mom managed to get the audible app installed on his phone and had downloaded some of the books in the library. I asked him if he was listening to any books. He said he was. My mind drew a blank, I couldn't remember what book he was listening to. I asked him if he had any requests. He said "yes." He requested books from original German philosophers in German. He had mentioned Bonhoeffer and Martin Luther. There was a pause before he added "I'd like the Bible in German."

While there was more to the conversation than just books on audible, I found myself in awe of my dad. He wanted to listen to books in German from German heroes of the Christian faith. A mind of a scholar and a heart for God, I thought to myself.

Dad Jokes

August 31, 2023 - Kat

I don't know if any of you have had the pleasure of experiencing my dad's "dad jokes" but it's a staple when I converse with him. I spoke to him earlier this morning and he decided to tell me a couple of jokes. Enjoy.

"What do you call an alligator in a vest? …. An investigator."

"Why are sledding dogs bad dancers? …They have two left feet."

"How do snowmen greet each other? …Ice to see you."

> **Harris:** This one's for Michael: "The walk from my house to the local tavern takes 5 minutes. The walk from the local tavern to my house takes 30 minutes. The difference is STAGGERING!" (I too have been diagnosed with a nasty case of dad jokes).

The Picture

Sept. 1, 2023 – Kat

Above my dad's reading/napping chair is a picture. It's the only picture in his office. In one of my moments while I was rummaging through his desk, I leaned back and glanced at that corner of the room. It hadn't struck me before but it did at that moment. It's an expression of Christ's blood spilled for the world. If there is anyone who can perform miracles, it's Christ.

The Weaver

In the last two days, Michael has seemed more communicative with fewer hiccups. Prayer and medication!

I have always loved this powerful poem by an unknown author.

The Weaver

> My life is but a weaving
> Between my Lord and me,
> I cannot choose the colors
> He worketh steadily.
>
> Oftimes He weaveth sorrow,
> And I in foolish pride
> Forget He sees the upper
> And I, the underside.
>
> Not till the loom is silent
> And the shuttles cease to fly
> Shall God unroll the canvas
> And explain the reason why.
>
> The dark threads are as needful
> In the Weaver's skillful hand
> As the threads of gold and silver
> In the pattern He has planned.

Dad's Agenda

Sept. 3, 2023 - Kat

"If anyone asks, tell them I have a screw loose in my head" my dad told me. "Let them know so they know what to pray for," he finished.

I was sipping coffee listening to my dad go about his agenda for tomorrow and beyond. He talked about launching a new branch of his work. He talked about traveling, "If I need to do this again, I'm going to travel with you or Mom." Agreed, you're not traveling alone again, I told myself. The conversation reminded me of a few days ago when I was at his desk.

After the phone call I made my way over to his office in order to find a piece of information my mom requested. A room saturated in books, and papers. I took a seat in his chair staring blankly at the monitors. Email boxes, and Facebook accounts were pulled up. I take a deep breath and proceed to recall a memory of him telling me where the document could be found. "Everything is in this folder," he said. I glanced at his desk. I sighed. I couldn't remember what that folder looked like. I start sifting through the pile of folders and papers: coaching, Coaching Suicide Awareness, S.U.N, Ethics, Convene, random pages of this and that. I eventually found the folder.

Before opening the folder, I took a moment and glanced at everything that was on the desk. Busy man, I thought. Busy changing the world.

The Coach with a Coach

Sept. 4, 2023 - Joy

This picture was taken last year when Michael first came to Bratislava to teach a coaching seminar. Michael and Marián, the local organizer of the seminar,  were visiting one of the castles previously owned by Michael's great grandfather. Michael thought it was amusing to be a coach standing next to a coach.

Today was a good day. Prayers and medication have greatly improved Michael's symptoms. He left the ICU and moved into a private room. The doctors are now allowing me to stay with him all day, which is actually quite miraculous. There are actually very strict regulations about visiting hours.

A foreign language can be a challenge. Trying to communicate with medical personnel solely through the phone's Google Translation App is an interesting experience. Consequently, it was like a breath of fresh air last week when a young woman orderly spoke to us in fluent English. She was very kind and helped us with some translations. Unfortunately, it was her last day to work at the hospital as school begins this week. Consequently, we were surprised and delighted when she walked into Michael's room this afternoon. After just a few minutes, she and Michael started talking about relationships. Michael the coach appeared. It is the essence of who he is. He loves helping people move forward in their lives, their businesses, their relationships.

Michael is a coach!

> *TJ:* Both the Royal coach and coach Michael are really the same because both are vehicles who take people from where they are to where they want to go. Isn't that the same as what Michael does?

The Little Things

Sept. 9, 2023 - Joy

All things are proceeding toward the operation on Thursday the 14th, which is our next prayer goal. Due to the reduction of some of the drugs, Michael has been very sleepy, and occasionally disoriented. He doesn't like the feeling of not being in control of his brain. After re-introducing some of the drugs, Michael became more lively and talkative yesterday evening.

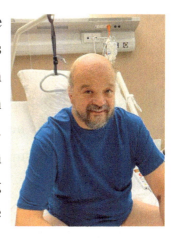

Sometimes we let the little things influence our mood and take our eyes off God and His desire to do great things in our lives. After an awesome week of prayer, little mosquitoes started irritating by buzzing around the heads of some of our prayer warriors trying to distract us from the blessings and answered prayers. (Sickness, obstacles, concerns) Ultimately God cares about the little things, as well as the big ones. For me those "mosquitoes" were batted aside yesterday. God reaffirmed that we are in the place He wants us to be for the surgery and for His glory.

Stand Firm

Sept. 10, 2023 - Joy

Content Warning: No medical updates...Just the ramblings of his wife.

Among the many advantages of Caring Bridge, these posts have become a way for me to process what is going on in our lives as well as the thoughts and spiritual paths this road is taking me on. So thanks for reading & listening to my ramblings. A few days ago, I wondered about sharing some of these thoughts. I then argued that people want updates on Michael, not a mini sermon from me. However, this is not just Michael's journey; it is also mine. The two of us as individuals became one almost 40 years ago, as Michael likes to tell the nursing staff. One nurse even demanded to know what year I was born since she didn't seem to believe the number.

Since I have been here in Bratislava, I have spent a lot of time on public transportation. It is a great place to pray and read. Even though I am usually an avid audio book reader, my audio novels have lost all appeal. I am only interested in praying and reading the Bible. Within the first day, God gave me a word, which I posted in the article entitled "Discouraging to Encouraging."

Those of you, who have made Jesus Christ the center of your lives, know that the Bible is God's living word. It is living because at times, through the power of the Holy Spirit, certain words, passages and promises will jump off the page and will hit you with such force that it practically takes your breath away. The Holy Spirit is then saying, "Today, this passage is for you!" That is exactly what happened with the verse I shared from Zechariah's prayer of praise in the above-mentioned post. Several days ago, I was reading the Lazarus story, which I have read and heard multiple times since childhood. This time, however, Jesus spoke directly to me when he said, "This sickness is for the glory of God. This happened to bring glory to the Son of God." John 11:4 Wow! So exciting! I wanted to shout it from the rooftops.

After speaking to a retired insurance agent, I became a bit concerned about our travel health insurance. A friend's prayer then spoke to me. "You (God) could have healed Michael outright but you have allowed this path for him. One that although asks him to endure suffering yet also is beyond question *covered by your provision of care.*" (Italics are mine.) The insurance company has not yet promised to pay the hospital, but I am no longer concerned.

As I already mentioned, I spend a lot of time on the bus. Since I was so into these contemplations today, I missed my connection. The shortest route to the hospital is bus - tram - bus. This morning I looked up as my last chance to catch the tram glided past my window. Oops! The alternative (bus - bus) is a little longer. I realized this is just like life! We can follow the path God has for us...or not. If I miss the stop accidentally, there is usually an alternative, but it may take longer. If I choose to reject God and His plan for my life, He will just find someone else to accomplish His plans.

I have often heard people say, "How can I believe in a God who would allow such bad things to happen?" I started thinking about Corrie ten Boom. She and her sister Betsie struggled through a horrible period of history. Betsie was a strong believer in being grateful for <u>all</u> things. (1 Thess. 5:18) At the time, Corrie couldn't believe that she should be grateful for the fleas in their Nazi concentration camp. However, the fleas kept the soldiers from discovering their hidden scriptures and their evening Bible study group. If you have never read the story of their lives, you should! I looked her up on the internet today in order to make sure that I spelled her name correctly. As an extra bonus, I found a number of her quotes, which have positively impacted me:

- When a train goes through a tunnel and it gets dark, you don't throw away the ticket and jump off. You sit still and trust the engineer.
- Never be afraid to trust an unknown future to a known God.
- Worry does not empty tomorrow of its sorrow, it empties today of its strength.

TJ: I love this quote from Corrie ten Boom, "Every trial that God gives us is the perfect preparation for a future that only He knows." What wisdom she had and positivity to keep going through such a horrific situation.

Message from Michael

Sept. 13, 2023 - Joy

The time has almost arrived for which we have been (mostly) patiently waiting. Michael's surgery is just a few hours away. It is scheduled for 8am on Thursday September 14, 2023 European time. Eastern Time: 2am, Mountain Time: Midnight. The surgery may take most of the day.

Thank you once again for your continued prayers.

Danke! D'akujem! Teşekkürler! Dank je! Gracias! Grazie!

Message from Michael

During this one time when people from around the world are listening, I want to share my heart with you. For whatever strange reason, I have been called to create a nonprofit called Coaching Suicide Awareness. Helping save lives is my greatest passion. This is my life's work.

Many people have asked what they can do for me. I have only one request. Visit our website. Choose a video presentation. Watch it and promote it, PLEASE. Post it on Facebook, Linked-In, anywhere. Get the message out. Help us save lives. I can't wait to watch the video done by Hannah Hadley. "A Teenager's Perspective on Passive Suicide Ideation." She has such a beautiful message. I am desperately concerned about suicide ideation of our teens. I am so proud and excited to promote these videos.

https://coachingsuicideawareness.com/

Mission: We provide networking and resources for suicide readiness training for professionals, including coaches who are dedicated to saving lives and bringing hope to those contemplating or affected by suicide. This spans all cultural, country, and age classifications.

From Joy: The 3rd eSummit, which Michael and many other volunteers organized, was an extremely powerful event which just occurred on Sept. 10-11, 2023. Unfortunately and for obvious reasons, Michael was not able to attend. Afterwards he was given a brief description of how powerful each of the speakers were. Even as Michael's wife, I have rarely seen him cry. As Michael listened to the description of the presentations, tears flowed freely down his face.

Good News, Bad News

Sept. 14, 2023 - Joy

Last night (the 13th) Michael was all prepared to go into surgery today for which we have all been praying. Suddenly he experienced an excruciating pain in his abdomen. After a few tests, the medical staff determined that Michael needed immediate emergency surgery. At midnight the surgical staff found and repaired the tear in his bowels. Michael is now resting comfortably in the ICU.

Good News: Michael's surgery went well and there were no complications.

Bad News: The surgeons opened up his abdomen instead of his brain.

Prayer Request: New surgical appointment for the brain tumor.

> ***Cathy:*** When you're in a boat in the storm, there's no telling when you'll get tossed around. Just remember, Jesus is in the boat with you; He's not concerned, keep trusting Him. Prayers for your faith and "faith-rest" in this uncertainty!

Cabinet Meetings

Sept. 14, 2023 - Kat

Fall of 2008, Germany, in the kitchen of our home

Like many nights, we end up gathering in the slender kitchen (slender by American standards) of the house. My dad was getting out the *Abendbrot* box (a box of cold cuts and cheese) and my mom was cleaning up. I took my place on the counter. We naturally began discussing the happenings of the day. At some point during the conversation my dad mentioned that our evening gatherings mirror that of a *cabinet meeting*. He explained that the term originated in England by politicians that gathered in the kitchen. A gathering of every member to plan and strategize. The details of his explanation escapes me. Over the years, this was a constant in our family. A gathering of all cabinet members to discuss and plan the next steps (I may be the only one that refers to it as a *cabinet meeting*).

yesterday, before the scheduled brain surgery and the emergency surgery

"I'm ok, I'm not nervous" my dad said. I wished I weren't nervous, I thought to myself. My dad goes on to talk a bit more about the procedure. "You know what I want" he paused, "I want to celebrate Thanksgiving and to celebrate me coming back." I heard him sniffle. "Let's do that," I barely replied. The conversation continued for a bit. My mind was thinking of everything and nothing. My heart was feeling everything and nothing. I recalibrated myself. "If anyone can make it through this, it would be you." I say. He giggled. I smiled. The conversation soon ended.

I was sitting in the kitchen looking at the shadows where the other cabinet members would be standing. Visualizing them here and not in Slovakia...Our meetings would typically end with a plan and one of us, if not all of us, saying "that's the plan." My heart weighing heavy against my chest, I absent mindedly nod and tell myself, "That's the plan..."

Surgical Appointments

Sept. 18, 2023 - Joy

Even though it is normally not easy to get surgical appointments for such delicate surgeries, our neurosurgeon visited this morning and reported that Michael is scheduled for brain surgery on Wednesday, September 20. Continuing to heal from his abdominal surgery is a prerequisite.

We appreciate all of the prayers, comments, Bible verses and good wishes. We have even received two songs as words of encouragement. **"Yes, I will"** is one of the songs, which I want to share.

https://youtu.be/NrTv39-lG4M?si=DCevmmXmffsjBQqr

> I count on one thing
> The same God that never fails
> Will not fail me now
> You won't fail me now
> In the waiting
> The same God who's never late
> Is working all things out
> You're working all things out

Yes, I believe that God is working all things out for the good. Even though we do not understand the additional surgery, pain and waiting, we know that God is in control of our lives and the circumstances.

> Yes I will, lift You high in the lowest valley
> Yes I will, bless Your name
> Oh, yes I will, sing for joy when my heart is heavy

I am reminded to praise and sing for joy even in the valley when my heart is heavy. These lyrics seem so appropriate.

Blessings

Sept. 19, 2023 - Joy

Brain surgery is scheduled for tomorrow, September 20. Praising that we have the earliest possible date. Praying that everything goes well in preparation for surgery and of course during the surgery. Praying also for the doctor's "decisions and incisions."

Michael's words, "God isn't finished with me yet. There is still more to accomplish for His glory. Lord, let me have the strength to do what You have called me to do."

I have felt guided and blessed during every step of this journey. It is not a path gladly chosen nor easily traversed. Most of the passage has been in a valley. We would much rather have already been hiking the road to recovery.

The 40-year sojourn of the Isrealites in the desert is a well-known story. When I was much younger, I wondered how the Isrealites could have seen all of God's miracles first hand and then doubted, complained and questioned when the going got tough. Arrogantly, I assumed that I would not have been like them. However, when you are reading the story with knowledge of the outcome, it is much easier to judge than when you are in the midst of the story with uncertainty ahead.

Therefore, I want to take a moment to look at all of the ways in which God has guided us and praise Him for the people He has put in our path:

- I purchased travel health insurance for Michael's trip.

- The flight to Europe significantly exacerbated Michael's symptoms leading to the discovery of the tumor. If he had not flown, who knows when or how the tumor would have been discovered.

- I was able to fly to Slovakia immediately as our daughter happened to be living with us and could take care of my dogs. Fortunately, this is one of the slower seasons for my business.

- Michael's friend and colleague took excellent care of Michael when he arrived. He and his wife have opened their home to us for as long as needed. They have been a wonderful local support.

- Michael's seminar attendee put us in touch with a well-known oncologist, who made connections with a great neurosurgeon. Michael's first doctor is also a friend of the neurosurgeon. All of these doctors have given me their private cell phone numbers, which is very unusual. (Multiple blessings!)

- Bratislava has a brand new hospital with all of the best equipment.

- People all over the world have been praying for Michael. There has been an incredible outpouring of prayer support.

- Michael has developed relationships with several of the medical professionals. Michael is especially passionate about helping and talking to young men such as William (Viliam) in the picture.

- A hospital administrator offered to let me spend the night with her family.

When you look at all of these little blessings, it creates a picture of assurance that we are where God wants us to be for this procedure.

> *Rick:* You can definitely see the fingerprints of the Almighty all over this journey!!

No complications

Sept. 20, 2023 - Joy

Michael's surgery went well with no complications! Fortunately the neurosurgeon contacted me directly as soon as he was finished with the surgery. Michael is in the ICU and plans to return to his room in the morning if all goes well. More updates to come. Thanks for your prayers!!

> *Elizabeth:* I can let my breath out now. I am reminded of Charlie Duke's (Apollo 11 CAPCOM) quote when the lunar module landed safely on the moon, "We copy you down Eagle. There's a bunch of guys turning blue out here!"

Rest & Peace & Healing

Sept. 22, 2023 - Joy

How is Michael? For two days he has had severe headaches. I guess that makes sense when you understand that a couple of people were rummaging around in that closet of a brain. They were just trying to throw out all of the trash. Michael is functioning well physically and cognitively, which is a huge answer to prayer.

The surgeons are pleased with the results. They showed us comparative pictures and the positive results in Michael's brain.

New Prayer Request: Rest & Peace & Healing

One of our friends put it so beautifully, "We pray for the brain to calm into a natural healing rhythm."

Release

Sept. 26, 2023 - Joy

Since the brain surgery, Michael has made significant steps towards recovery. After 30 days in two hospitals, which included two very serious surgeries, Michael couldn't wait to walk (or hobble) out the  hospital door. After convincing the doctors that he could and would rest and heal better at our friend's village home and garden, the doctors finally gave us permission to leave. What a pleasure to breathe the fresh air and feel the sun's rays on your head. These are some of the little things, which we often take for granted. The morning flew by with various last minute check-ups, a variety of paperwork, and a number of prescriptions.

The only things, which currently steal his joy, are the nagging, persistent headaches. Please pray that the headaches disappear. I would like prayer that we can both get into a normal sleep rhythm. Sleeping all day and then buzzing with energy and a desire to "do something" in the wee hours of the morning is exhausting for both of us.

The Little Engine That Could

Sept. 30, 2023 - Kat

Winter of 2008 Germany. In the living room of our house.

I was walking down the hall feeling sad and somewhat defeated. I don't remember what caused it but as a teenager at the time anything would have triggered the emotion. I stopped by my room but quickly decided to walk on further to my father's study/living room. I went straight for the couch and planted myself face down on the nearest pillow. My dad swirled around on his chair to face me. "What's wrong?" he asked. I remained silent for a few long pauses then spoke. He listened. When I had stopped, he said "You know what you need, a good story." He added, "This is an American classic." My dad had mentioned on a few occasions wanting to read me that story. I guess now posed the best opportunity for him to finally do so. He picked a book off the shelf and turned to me. *The Little Engine That Could* He opened the book, and with the enthusiasm of a kindergarten teacher began reading to me.

*Today

I woke up to my mother's message, "Dad is being readmitted into the hospital." My heart dropped. I had just established a plan for my parents' arrival on Sunday. I was filled with hope laced with a hint of anxiety. The news sent me back into numbness. I called my mother, no answer. My heart started racing, and my mind was in a panic. Taming the urge not to be mad at God, I worked on readjusting my perspective. My mother returns my calls. "He's been diagnosed with sepsis," she stated. "He's been given antibiotics," she assured me. My dad interjected and said, "My mom died from sepsis." He was laying in the bed, eyes barely open. "We're not flying tomorrow," he added. I shared my disappointment at the reality. "How are you feeling?" I asked. He tilted his hand indicating that he was feeling so-so. I made feeble attempts at humor. The call was cut short.

"So close," I told myself as I aimlessly walked through the house. My wandering took me to my father's office. I glanced at his bookshelf. The same bookshelf that had been set up in Germany. I scan his collection of books; *The Case For Faith, Environment of International Business, Learning To Listen, Karl Marx, 10x For Christ, Die Zehn Gebote*...my eyes land on a familiar book. I pull it out of its place. *The Little Engine That Could.*' I hear him talk in my head. I stood there recalling a plethora of his nuggets of wisdom he has imparted to me throughout the years. This being one of them. Tears fell. Dancing between hope and despair, I skim through the book pausing at the last few pages...

"puff, puff, chug, chug, went the Little Blue Engine. 'I think I can- I think I can- I think I can- I think I can- I think I can-' Up, up, up. Faster and faster and faster the little engine climbed, until at last they reached the top of the mountain."

-The Little Engine That Could

Going Home

Oct. 4, 2023 - Joy

Finally, we are on our way home. We left the hospital this afternoon. We are packed and ready to head towards the airport at 4am

Requesting prayers for:

Michael's headaches - They continue to be quite severe.

A smooth flight - Good connections and no adverse effects with the pressure changes

A positive transition to care in the USA upon our return.

We will keep you all informed.

THANKS SO MUCH for your love, encouragement and support.

Precious Cargo

Oct. 5, 2023 - Kat

My father was situated in the passenger's seat, as my mother was adjusting herself in the back seat. I start to drive the last leg of their itinerary. A few minutes into the drive my mother says, "He's sensitive to sharp turns and bumps." I nod. This shouldn't be too difficult. A few more  minutes go by. I received a message from my uncle. Odd. He usually doesn't text. I pull up the message on the car screen, "Precious cargo aboard. Drive extra carefully," it read. I looked at my dad. I couldn't read him. I don't know if he was happy, sad, in pain, tired, hungry, thirsty? No idea. What I do know is that he was 'precious cargo.' I drove with extra awareness of potholes, dips and sharp curves. Everything went well until we got to our driveway. Gravel, bumps and sharp turns all the way up to the house. My father vocalized discomfort, and I did my best to make the ride as easy on his body as possible. We made it to the top of the hill. We got him inside. He took his place on the coach and said, "Thank you Jesus."

A battle was won today, and while I should appreciate the moment of this event, I know more are heading our way.

173

Bittersweet

Oct. 9, 2023 - Kat

My dad likes chocolate, particularly dark chocolate. During my parents' stay in Slovakia, my mom had taken some contraband dark chocolate into the hospital. *Such a rebel.* Once they were homebound, I was gifted with four different varieties of dark chocolate they had savored during their stay there.

Dark chocolate supposedly helps with lowering stress levels and is considered all around "healthy," or so they say. My stress levels are currently high. Seems like a good time to sample the souvenir.

Update:

Since being home, my father has continued to have mind-splitting headaches. An expected side effect from his recent brain surgery. He is currently struggling with vision, memory, orientation and other physiological and psychological aspects. Despite efforts to expedite my father's intake with the oncologist, foreign documents and foreign confidentiality regulations have had us moving at turbo snail mail velocity. My mother and I grew concerned and decided we couldn't wait for paperwork to arrive and took him to the ER today.

They arrived at the hospital around 12:30 pm, he was given a bed around 3:00 pm, my dad had an MRI scan done and around 7-ish in the evening my mom called me.

"They want to fly him out to Colorado Springs. Tonight."

Huh? What just happened?! The plan was to get him radiation treatment for his second tumor. I thought loudly to myself.

The doctor came into their room. After a brief discussion, we decided to fly him out to Colorado Springs.

I blankly stare at the bar of chocolate on the table. I hadn't really noticed that I've been eating away at the chocolate bar a lot quicker than I care to admit. I break off another square. My thoughts move from my head, to my heart, then to my taste buds. *Bittersweet...much like this moment.*

Crescendo

Oct. 12, 2023 - Kat

I was assisting my father into bed, after their drive back from Colorado Springs. I laid the blanket on top of him. As he lay there, I noticed the hospital bracelets around his wrists. I attempted humor, "Looks like you went to several concerts." He looks over to his wrists. "It does," he says as he tries to smile.

Update on my father:

It was determined that he has glioblastoma. Apparently, it was important for hospitals in the US to confirm the pathology report from the hospital in Slovakia. A referral had been sent out for radiation treatment. His first appointment is this coming Monday. We don't know if it's a consultation appointment or actual treatment. He is still struggling with the things I had mentioned in the previous post.

Update on my mother:

What was a two person run household has consolidated into one. Responsibilities that my father would shoulder have all of the sudden fallen on my mother. Her job of late is making sense of the chaos that couldn't be addressed while overseas. On top of keeping everything a float, which she and my father had set out to do, she is tired, wired, restless, and stressed.

Overall:

"One step at a time" is what we would advise each other when things get tough. We try to keep that in mind. So far, we try to include my father with family decision making (as much as we can.) We do our best to help him and to make him comfortable. I'm no musician but I would describe our current situation as a *crescendo* in a long symphony with no idea of how long the song will play.

Man's Chief Aim

Oct. 17, 2023 - Joy

The focal point of our lives since the end of August has been the brain tumors, which have caused 42 nights in three hospitals, two major surgeries, four trips to emergency rooms, and one night flight.

Even though our whole life has recently revolved around this little mass in the center of Michael's brain, he was not at first completely cognizant of the fact that having a brain tumor meant having cancer. The official Slovakian pathology report, which

176

Google helped me translate into English, confirmed the existence of glioblastoma.

GBMResearch.org:

> "Glioblastoma is a highly malignant form of cancer that affects the brain… It is non-genetic in nature and develops quickly. The reasons for its occurrence are unknown. There is no cure for Glioblastoma. Treatments focus on removing or shrinking the tumor to reduce symptoms; however, they are not successful in long-term survival, making Glioblastoma a devastating diagnosis with most patients surviving an average of 12 to 18 months after diagnosis."

In the last post, Kat referred to the multiple hospital wristbands indicating name, allergy, fall risk, and DNR. Kat wanted to cut off all of these wristbands, but Michael insisted on keeping the DNR band (Do Not Resuscitate). From the beginning of this medical excursion, Michael has continually informed the medical professionals of his DNR desires. As Christians, many often quote the verse from Philippians 1:21, "To live is Christ, to die is gain." Personally, I have never quite been able to wrap my mind around this verse. However, I found a translation of this verse, which makes more sense to me and seems to embody Michael's perspective.

> The Passion Translation of Philippians 1:21-24, "My true life is the Anointed One, and dying means gaining more of him. So here's my dilemma: Each day I live means bearing

more fruit in my ministry; yet I fervently long to be liberated from this body and joined fully to Christ. That would suit me fine, but the greatest advantage to you would be that I remain alive. So you can see why I'm torn between the two—I don't know which I prefer."

For Michael, dying holds no fear. He is looking forward to spending eternity with Christ. Yet, he wants to make each day count for Christ. I see a new passion in Michael to make each day count and to take nothing for  granted. A kiss from a dog and an excursion to Walmart are experiences he treasures. It was actually an accomplishment to push the Walmart cart on his own. Not only does he want to enjoy

every day, he wants to bring joy to others. He encouraged the manager of a fast food restaurant, told a stranger that he liked her smile, and talked to the UPS driver about long-lasting marriages. He is reaching out to strangers even more than before.

Today Michael said, "Man's chief aim is to glorify God and enjoy Him forever."

Next week Michael will start a combination of radiation and chemotherapy. I am praying that God heals him and extends his life. Michael said, "God can heal me. He is a God of the impossible!" Whether or not God heals him, Michael is content.

The New Normal?

Oct. 26, 2023 - Joy

My dogs and I are both excited about having two dog cart tours this week. After a two-month break, they were anxious to run. It is good to get back to our normal routine. But what is normal?

Michael is very grateful that the headaches have gone away. We praise God for an answer to prayer. We also know that the steroids have helped eliminate the headaches. Michael is also walking, talking and functioning better on steroids.

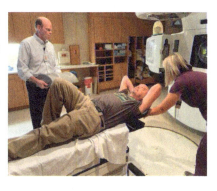

Michael's new normal consists of daily trips to Durango for radiation treatments. Durango is about an hour and a half from our house. We have been blessed with several friends who are sharing the driving responsibilities. The radiation process is fascinating. There is a specially made face mask which keeps his head immobilized. Then the radiation is precisely targeted to the specific areas of the brain which needs it. In conjunction with the radiation, chemotherapy in the form of nightly pills are taken. Having just started this process this week, we haven't yet noticed side effects. The doctors warn that chemotherapy can cause the loss of hair. Michael's response: "What hair?"

Ebenezer

Nov. 11, 2023 - Joy

As we slowly head into the Christmas season, many of you may have thought of Ebenezer Scrooge when you saw the title of this post. However, the Hebrew name Ebenezer is actually based on  Samuel 7 and means "stone of help." The dictionary even defines the word as "a commemoration of divine assistance." When we purchased our first house in Germany, Michael felt very strongly about giving God the glory for accompanying us through life's journey. He had the words Eben-Eser (German spelling) engraved in marble and mounted on our new home. The plaque has followed us ever since and is still mounted on the corner of our house.

God is continuing to guide and accompany us even along this rough path. Michael continues radiation therapy five times a week accompanied by daily chemotherapy pills, which continues through the beginning of December. I am beginning to notice some of the negative side effects of the treatment. Our daughter Kat summed it up, "He is functional yet he is not; he is insightful and reflective yet not. His executive function is damaged and so is his emotional regulation. It's an expected side effect."

We are very grateful for the volunteers who are driving Michael to his daily appointments located 1.5 hours from our home. We are also very thankful to all who have contributed to our financial situation. We thank Michael's company Convene who set up a page through Helping Hands.

(https://hhmin.org/charities/michael-marx/) All of you have been such a blessing to us.

Michael continues to appreciate and value every day. He is determined to "Make Every Day Count" as it says on his new t-shirt. His personal mission and current calling is to speak to everyone he meets and remind them to appreciate their loved  ones. He has called many of you to express how much you mean to him. He values all of you! If you haven't received a call, it is probably because your number is not programmed into his cell phone.

One day we were walking out of the hospital after his treatment. Unusually an elderly man spoke to Michael first. After talking for a few minutes about life and marriage, Michael said, "I have been married for 40 years. The one word I use to describe our marriage is 'devotion.' You have been married for 68 years. What one word would you say helped you stay married for 68 years?" The man thought about it, looked up and responded:

"Yes, ma'am!"

Functional Medicine

Nov. 19, 2023 - Joy

God has once again blessed us by bringing a functional medicine doctor into our lives, who is willing to donate his time and expertise. His suggested reading material is high on our list of priorities. (Joel Fuhrman's *Eat for Life*, Michael Greger's *How Not To Die*, and Nathan Crane's *Becoming Cancer Free*.) We have learned a lot about how  fruit, vegetables, nuts, seeds and beans are the primary foods, which provide the body with the best nutrients to fight cancer and other diseases. Michael has already (mostly) eliminated sugar from his diet, which cancer cells love to consume.

We wish you all a blessed Thanksgiving celebration this week. We are grateful to be home and alive. Thank you for your continued prayers.

Limbo

Jan. 1, 2024 - Joy

I feel like we are in a state of limbo. Limbo: What an odd word. As I thought about it, I even wondered if it was accurate. So I looked up the definition, "an uncertain period of awaiting a decision or resolution; an intermediate state or condition." Yep. Accurate.

The radiation and chemotherapy treatments have ended yet the next MRI isn't scheduled until January 17. The radiologist wants to give Michael's brain time to recover from the treatments. Our functional medicine doctor has done extensive blood work and has recommended many supplements designed to reduce inflammation and rid Michael's body of the toxins and heavy metals found in his blood. All of this takes time. Michael is requesting prayer for relief from the chemo fog, which continues to cause fatigue and disorientation.

Michael is recovering by reading, praying, and talking with many of you on the phone. Thank you for your continued prayers for him and for me. Michael has told me how many of you have asked about me and are praying for my strength during my busiest time of the year. (Dog sled tours during the Christmas holidays.)

Recently Laura Story's song Blessings has been constantly playing in my head. I want to share this song with you. Maybe it will touch you in the way it has me. Laura's husband was also diagnosed with a brain tumor. Her song seems to originate from a similar situation of pain and prayer.

Blessings by Laura Story

https://www.youtube.com/watch?v=XQan9L3yXjc

We pray for blessings

We pray for peace

Comfort for family, protection while we sleep

We pray for healing, for prosperity

We pray for Your mighty hand to ease our suffering

And all the while, You hear each spoken need Yet love is

way too much to give us lesser things

'Cause what if your blessings come through raindrops?

What if Your healing comes through tears?

What if a thousand sleepless nights

Are what it takes to know You're near?

And what if trials of this life are Your mercies in disguise?

We pray for wisdom

Your voice to hear

And we cry in anger when we cannot feel You near

We doubt Your goodness, we doubt Your love

As if every promise from Your Word is not enough

And all the while, You hear each desperate plea

And long that we'd have faith to believe

Cause what if your blessings come through raindrops?

What if Your healing comes through tears?

And what if the thousand sleepless nights

Are what it takes to know You're near?

And what if trials of this life are Your mercies in disguise?

When friends betray us
And when darkness seems to win
We know that pain reminds this heart
That this is not, this is not our home
It's not our home

Cause what if your blessings come through raindrops?
What if Your healing comes through tears?
And what if the thousand sleepless nights
Are what it takes to know You're near?

What if my greatest disappointments
Or the aching of this life
Is the revealing of a greater thirst this world can't satisfy
And what if trials of this life
The rain, the storms, the hardest nights
Are Your mercies in disguise?

Date Days

Jan. 17, 2024 - Joy

Instead of "date nights," Michael and I have recently had "date days." Since we had to go to the "big city" of Durango (population 19,000) for treatment, we then visit a store or restaurant. One day we found ourselves in Denny's for a late lunch. We started looking at all of the old couples enjoying a meal at this American diner.

Then we looked at ourselves and realized that we were also one of the "old couples." A sobering thought.

We have been waiting for and many people have been praying for this date (Jan. 17th) for the last 6 weeks. Today's MRI was compared to the one done in October when we first returned home from Slovakia. As the radiologist said today, "In the scope of what we could be seeing, this result is fairly good." There is less swelling in Michael's brain. No significant growth in the tumor on the occipital lobe has occurred. Considering that this form of cancer (Glioblastoma) is a very aggressive, fast-growing type, the doctors consider this MRI to be fairly good and the situation to be "largely stable."

Seeds of Hope

Jan. 24, 2024 - Joy

So many people have asked about me and are praying for me as well as for Michael. I want to take a minute to once again thank all of you who pray for us. Over the last few months, I have shouldered more than I thought was physically and emotionally possible, especially in the midst of my busiest season, the Christmas holidays. Your prayers have sustained me.

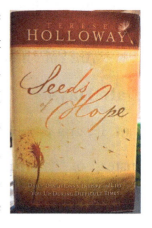

A lady from church put this book *Seeds of Hope* into my hands. Even though I don't usually read poetry, these daily devotional poems have been a real inspiration to Michael and me. I highly recommend this book. Yesterday, I read the following poem, which I have read multiple times from two different perspectives: of the burdened and of the intercessor. The poem reminds me of how many people are holding me up in prayer. THANK YOU, prayer warriors! You are helping me to bear this burden.

Called to Bear a Burden

Called to Bear a Burden, she fell upon her knees;
Feeling hopelessly alone, completely robbed of inner peace.
She dared not to imagine, this heartache to its depth;
For fear, she would stop breathing and take her final breath.
The intensity of pain rumbled deep within her soul;
It grabbed her like a vice, with no plan of letting go.
Oh, how she longed for Jesus and HIS peace within her pain;
So, she bowed her heart to heaven and she called upon His Name.
She received His reassurance, that she would make it through;
But she'd been called to Bear a Burden, and intercede for YOU!
For a moment, God removed, what He knew YOU could not bear;
And He placed it on another, who would lift you up in prayer.
It's just HIS way of showing, His depth of love for you;
In the midst of inner turmoil and this place He's called you to.
Yes, He lifts your heavy load, dispersing evenly its weight;
He carries you on other's wings, and helps you in life's race.
So, when you FEEL forsaken, remember--God's STILL there;
And He's calling burden-bearers, to intercede for YOU--in prayer!

Fatigue

Feb. 3, 2024 - Joy

We were delighted to spend some time with our 9-year old grandson, who was visiting from Florida. Michael even enjoyed losing a game of chess.

Currently fatigue is a big issue and a main prayer request. Michael would really like to have more energy. According to one journal article, "Fatigue has even been rated as being more troublesome than other symptoms, such as pain or nausea and vomiting, which can generally be managed by medications. Cancer Related Fatigue can also have profound psychosocial, and economic impacts. Despite the importance of fatigue in quality of life among patients with malignancy, it is well established that fatigue has been under-reported, underdiagnosed and undertreated."

The amount of time Michael spends "resting" is directly proportionate to the amount of time he spends in prayer. Michael has collected prayer requests from many of you, and he spends a considerable amount of time interceding on your behalf.

Hospice

For those of us who have never had to deal directly with hospice, the word sounds like a home or hospital into which terminal patients go to die. However, I have learned that "hospice" is a medical designation, not a location.

Hospice is "a program that gives special care to people who are near the end of life and have stopped treatment to cure or control their disease. Hospice offers physical, emotional, social, and spiritual support for patients and their families."

With much prayer, consideration and medical consultation, we have decided that hospice is the next step for Michael. Since January Michael has been experiencing increasingly severe headaches and nausea. Other previous symptoms of tumor growth are also resurfacing.

"Hospice care prioritizes comfort and quality of life by reducing pain and suffering." Today we should be receiving a package of drugs, which will better help deal with the symptoms than the ones I have on hand. Michael's care will now be overseen by a qualified nurse who will come to our home.

Rick: Scott Sauls quoted a conversation with a suffering friend in his book, *Irresistible Faith* - I asked how he could face such suffering with an admirable poise, & he replied "I've been a Bible reader all my life. Somewhere along the way, I guess it all sank in." A Bible that's falling apart usually belongs to someone who isn't. I can only imagine what your Bibles look like! Connecting in the pain is God's way. One thing Christians can do that the world can't do is suffer in joy, which is SO how you're each choosing to face this season. Jerry Sitter, in his *A Grace Disguised*, said, "It is not what happens to us that matters as much as what happens in us. Sorrow enlarges the soul until it is capable of simultaneously mourning & rejoicing." I join Jerry & you with the thought: Instead of asking "Why me?" ask "Why not me?" Thank you for the grace, trust & love you're both modeling to so many of us when WE want to be modeling that for each of YOU.

Bill: Michael, you have brought encouragement to so many that have received the truth from a man who is facing eternity with grace and hope. I am honored to know you and blessed by your courage and strength. Please pray that we might all have a faith like yours when the day approaches. In Christ, the solid rock you stand!

Commemorations

April 4, 2024 - Fred & Elizabeth

Michael worked long and hard to become someone who could benefit people. He became a global subject matter expert positioned to multiply the good. His individual counseling brought greater productivity. His group leadership, whether in athletics or in suicide prevention awareness, inspired progress. Michael did not wait to earn a title, gain permission, or hold fast to one direction... he led from where he was.

Michael's faith served as his foundation and motivation. He believed in putting out his best work on a path he knew his God would appreciate.

The body will fail us all someday. That day will be sooner for Michael, so we siblings would like to celebrate him while he might still be uplifted by it.

The Path

April 21, 2024 - Joy

First of all, I am overwhelmed by the outpouring of comments, greetings, prayers, well-wishes, cards, stories, and commemorations in response to the last post as well as all of those received along this journey. Michael's siblings, who are both older and didn't grow up with him, have indicated that they have gotten to know him much better through your words. THANK YOU! Michael has also told me that he wants to thank each of you and express how grateful he is that you are in his life. He would like to write a bunch of cards expressing these sentiments. Unfortunately, he is no longer capable of writing cards, so as a family we say, "Thank you and God Bless You All."

Michael has received some special gifts. Since he easily gets very cold, these blankets, prayer shawls, and quilts have been well used. Each prayer said for Michael is greatly appreciated. Praying for others is a wonderful ministry.

Personally, I am awed by how many people are also praying for me and have also shown so much concern about my health and stamina. So, in answer to the typical question, "How are you?" my answer so far has been, "ok." ...Not great (obviously), but ok. I know what I have to do and eventually accomplish. As a task-oriented person, I feel that I can tackle most things one step at a time. I also consider myself to be a fairly patient person. (A very necessary trait for a caregiver) Maybe God felt that I could handle this situation. My grandfather used to say, "God doesn't give a person more than he can handle." Next came the punchline. "But I just wish He didn't have such a high estimation of my ability." (Haha)

For the last eight months, I have been ok... until this week. Even with additional fuel, the tank eventually runs dry. My empty tank is not a pleasant sight. I am physically weak and emotionally tired. My patience fled without informing me of its return. Tears overflow. Grief squeezes my heart. In spite of all of this, or maybe because of it, there have been many blessings and encouragements, which I want to share:

- A grief counselor contacted me and offered therapy without charge.
- Many people have volunteered their time to stay with Michael when I am unable to.
- Even though I couldn't attend church, God led me to an online service which had just the right message for me.
- A song "accidentally" popped up on YouTube with amazing lyrics.
- An old friend called with encouragement.
- Another friend forwarded Rick Warren's story of his son's suicide.

I could continue. These are just a few that have affected me and started refilling my tank today.

So if you have ever experienced pain or wanted to ask why God would allow … to happen, I highly recommend watching Rick Warren's interview. (Author of The Purpose Driven Life) It's only about 10 minutes:

https://www.youtube.com/watch?v=HCUbog65dP4

The song I discovered today for the first time is Shane & Shane Psalm 46. The chorus is very powerful.

https://www.youtube.com/watch?v=PKs_gQecaDY

Lord of Hosts, You're with us
With us in the fire
With us as a shelter
With us in the storm
You will lead us
Through the fiercest battle
Oh, where else would we go
But with the Lord of Hosts

All through the Bible a multitude of stories describe trial, pain and difficulties. God doesn't promise us an easy path, but He will walk with us when we ask Him to.

Heaven Bound

April 30, 2024 - Joy

Recently Michael's most sincere desire was to move on to the next phase of existence: Heaven & Everlasting life with his Savior Jesus Christ. I am very grateful that he did not have to linger on this earth. He was becoming impatient for this transition. Knowing that he was losing his physical abilities as well as some of his cognitive abilities made life very frustrating.

Often as people get older, the inner self becomes more apparent. It's as if the inner self exhibits itself to the world. One of my grandmothers became irritable and judgmental. My grandfather on the other side became super sweet and kind in spite of the stroke, which robbed him of his ability to speak. It has been wonderful to watch Michael's focus to be on serving others during this phase.

For a while Michael encouraged every stranger who crossed his path to express love to their family and friends. He was an encouragement to total strangers. He created a prayer map and became a serious intercessor. Even in his dreams, he tried to find ways to give to others, especially the homeless. He talked to me about starting a soup kitchen. (An endeavor which is far beyond my capabilities.) In his professional life, I estimate that he gave away 50% of his time to people and organizations.

Even in death he wanted to give. Knowing that the body is an empty shell once the spirit leaves, the leftover body was of no importance to him. Donating his organs, however, was very important to him. Michael wanted to make such an early departure from this world worthwhile. He wanted someone to get use out of body parts he could no longer use. Unfortunately, as I investigated the procedure for such donations, it became apparent that donating your organs is not very easy to do. There is a precise procedure, for which most deaths do not qualify. Consequently, he chose to donate his whole body to science. We were both impressed with Science Care.

(https://www.sciencecare.com/)

I want to thank all of you for accompanying us on this journey. You have sustained us with your prayers and well-wishes.

A Nugget of Wisdom

Joy: Michael wrote several short Nugget stories, some of which were published in our local newspaper *The Pagosa Sun*. Others have been published in a local magazine. I have been impressed with his ability to write a short amusing story and then leave the reader with something to think about or reflect on. These stories are worth sharing.

Nugget is a member of the Mountain Paws Dog Sledding team. She is a 13-year-old white furred Alaskan Husky with one bent ear. She loves to pull with her sister Poke. They were named after a gold-digger theme. She has run in the Alaskan Interior, the Herbert  Glacier, and now the San Juan Mountains of Colorado. Her ghostwriter is Michael J. Marx, EdD.

Born to pull

My name is Nugget and I'm a sled dog. The musher shouts: "Ready, let's go." The mountain hills unfold before us. The sun sparkles in the crisp, cold Colorado air.

"Gee" We turn towards the right. "Haw" We take the trail to the left.

We are running. We are pulling. Our blood pulses with song and energy. We can do this ALL DAY – like 100 miles per day. We are a dogsled team.

Smart ones in the front. Not so smart ones in the back. I run in the middle of the pack. We each have our jobs. The first two dogs run *lead* and obey our musher's commands. The next two are called *swing dogs* and reinforce the direction. Then come the *team* dogs. We keep the gang line tight. Just in front of the sled are the *wheel* dogs. They don't have to think. They just pull. We all have jobs. We all have skills. We all live to pull.

Paws to consider:

What are you made for?

Are you made

> to pull?
> to explore?
> to love?
> to lead?

What are you born to do?

The Lead Dog Sets the Pace

My name is Nugget and I'm a sled dog. I'm the self-appointed blogger of the team.

The lead dogs set the pace when they hear the musher call.

"Up, up!" means speed up.

"Easy, easy!" means trot, don't run.

"Whoa, whoa!" means stop.

The musher puts two dogs in the front row. Sometimes three. Sometimes one. They are responsible for setting the pace. A gangline connects us. If we tried to run faster than the leaders, there would be a big mess. A ball-up. The dog behind us gets his feet in our faces. The tug lines get wrapped around our legs. The dog in front of us sits on your head. It's no fun. I've been there many times.

I run in the middle of the pack next to Poke, my sister. Understanding commands is not my job. The leaders do that. We run at the speed the musher wants. If the whole team runs too fast, the driver stands on the brakes. In fact, that's what  happens most of the time. Left to our own devices we would run, run, run. We would run as hard as we could until someone keels over.

Paws to Consider:

Do you know how fast to run? Does someone help you keep pace?

Are you going   too fast?

                 too slow?

                 too recklessly?

Who helps you stay under control?

Step to the front

My name is Nugget, and I'm a sled dog.

"Okay, Nugget. It looks like you get to lead the team now."

The musher's words made little sense to me. Yet when the lead dog got a tummy ache, it became clear that she would run in the middle, and I would run in the front.

I had only been put in the lead position once before. I did not like it. Me being the lead dog did not go well. There was no dog ahead of me to follow. I did not know how to keep the gang line straight. I kept looking backward to the middle of the team, where I belonged. When it was time to go, I just sat down and refused. *Nope, I'm not a lead dog. Not gonna do it.*

Hmm, this time is different. Only five dogs on the team today. I am in front. No neck line. Just a tug line. Everyone depends on me to pull the team, to keep things straight, and to lead the pack. It is paramount for the lead dog to "tow the line." Hmm. What if I'm given a command like "gee" or "haw"? I'm not totally sure which way is right and which is left. Maybe I should pretend to have a tummy ache.

"Ready, let's go." That's the command to start. Reflexively I lunge forward. To my surprise, everyone follows. I pull. I follow the trail. The beaten path. I've been this way before. I know it. I can do this. We run at a slow, yet steady pace. After a little while, I led the team back to the dog truck. Yay! I did it. The musher is very happy with me. I'm happy with myself. Whew! I just don't want to do this every time.

Paws to consider:

Are you ready to step forward when needed?

Are you afraid of   forgetting the way?

                        failing the boss?

                        falling down?

Well, you know if you fall, fall forward; at least you're making progress.

What will you do when it's up to you to lead?

In the Dog House

My name is Nugget and I'm a sled dog.

Sometimes we can't wait to get going. My sled-dog partners and I are all hooked up to the sled and the humans are just talking. Humans do that a lot. Talk, talk, talk.

For sled dogs, it's run, run, run.

I get impatient and I start chewing on something. A neckline. A tugline. This time it was the gangline. This was really bad, because when I chewed through it, the four dogs in front of me were unattached. Eager to go, they took off down the trail... and without me!

"Stop," the guests in the sled yelled. That ain't gonna happen. Sled dogs run. Unabated they will run until something stops them... like a moose, or a pack of wolves. They were running out of control, reckless, and without regard for anything but speed. This is particularly dangerous because one of them could trip and turn upside down. The others might not stop. The topsy-turvy dog could get seriously injured like this.

Well, the quick-thinking musher jumped on the snowmobile and caught the renegade dogs. Phew! Saved. By the time she came back to me, I knew I was in the dog house.

She picked up the end of the frayed gang line and shoved it at my nose.

"Nugget! No. No! Bad dog."

Ouch, *bad dog* is the absolute worst thing to hear. I hung my head in shame. Maybe I can learn to curb my urges. Maybe I can learn to stay calm and be patient. That's hard when all I want is to run. It's not about me. I have to do what's best for the team. I have to learn to be still when required.

Paws to consider:

Are you able to be still?

Can you be   patient?

                      calm?

                      willing to wait?

Can you be ready to go and stand still at the same time?

Let me work

My name is Nugget and I'm a sled dog.

The man in the sled basket kept yelling, "You're doing a great job. Keep it up!"

What is this man saying? I look back at him trying to figure out what he means. The musher stops the convoy of two dog sleds and comes and checks on me.

We then continue to pull the sleds down the trail. The man again yells things I don't understand. I look back. The musher again stops and checks my paws, and shoulders.

The third time, it happened again. The musher explains to the old man in the sled-basket and the driver of the sled that when a dog keeps looking back, it usually means something is wrong.

"Well, I just keep yelling words of encouragement at them," says the passenger.

The musher admonishes him, "Oh! Ah, you're confusing them. They expect commands, not chatter. When you yell at them, say something like 'straight ahead!' Please."

How often are we distracted from our work? Well-meaning people do things that keep us from focusing on pulling the sleds. We can't hear the real commands from the noise. Do humans not know that sled dogs want to work? Doing what we are made to do is enough for us. We do not need someone to praise us for doing our jobs.

Paws to consider:

Are you able to do your work without distractions?

Can you be   quiet?
                  attentive?
                  single-minded?

What can you do to be more focused on your work?

Join Me in a Howl

My name is Nugget and I'm a sled dog

Ah-woo! I love to howl.

Ah-ah-ah-wooo!

I howl to say who I AM. Howling expresses my sense of being a dog. I don't howl to send any particular message. The other dogs around me like to join in. We quickly form a chorus of loud love for life.

Join me right now. Tilt back your head, let the sound of your heart flow through you, and saturate the night with your energy. Let the moon draw you.

Ready? Let's go: Ah-woooo. Ah-wooo. Arf. Arf. Ah-woo!

Dogs for miles around join us. Every creature great and small knows tonight dogs sing the sound of their feelings. They can be happy, sad, lonely, excited, disappointed, or just BE. Others will join in affirmation and add to the cacophony of life.

What's that? Oh, it's the musher yelling, "Quiet, Nugget quiet!"

How does the musher know that I usually start up the choir? "Nugget, no. BE QUIET!"

I've never understood her aversion to our music. Other humans turn on the lights on their porches and come out to try to make us stop. They can get quite upset.

Oh, well. The howling was fun while it lasted. I am more at peace. I feel more like a dog. I am dog – hear me howl!

Paws to consider:

How often do you want to let yourself go – to shout, sing, and yell?

Can you be   loud?

                     expressive?

                     comfortable in your own skin?

When was the last time you howled?

My Special Day

My name is Nugget and I'm a sled dog.

The night is just starting to get dark. The musher is coming out to the yard with that deliberate walk. I think she'll pick one of us to come inside for the night.

Pick me! Pick me. Yup. Yup. I'm the one.

She lets me loose and I waste no time running to the front door.

Oh, yes. I get to sleep on a soft bed tonight. Yup. Yup. Yup. I get treats and ear scratches. Yup. Yup.

I don't know whether I actually prefer sleeping outside or inside. I just know it's great to be chosen. This makes me feel special. Like I'm part of the family. Sometimes two or three of us get to come inside at the same time. I've noticed that the musher's husband is never at home when this happens. Hmm?

Inside they have a piece of juicy meat for me with a candle on it. They sing something. I just want to gulp that thing down. Get that silly candle out of the way. It doesn't taste good anyway and the flame scares me.

Yup. Yup. Gulp! The whole thing in one swallow. Yummy.

Paws to consider:

What do you like to have done for you on your special day?

Can you   run around at will?

                   eat anything you want?

                   do nothing if you want?

How do you celebrate the special folks in your life?

The CFO - Chief Fun Officer

My name is Nugget and I'm a sled dog.

Ah, there Timber goes again. He's on his back and Brooklyn has him by his thick furry neck and is shaking him violently. Of course, this looks to me like he is about to die.

I can't watch it. His legs go limp. Wait! He just jumped up, ran around, and came back for more. Jeez. I wish he were that enthusiastic about pulling a sled.

Timber and Brooklyn are Siberian Huskies. Unlike us Alaskan Huskies, they enjoy playing more than working. Mostly he keeps pace with the team yet doesn't pull all that much on the tug line. He doesn't pull his own weight so to speak. Yet as a people pleaser, he takes the cake (or the cookie). So, we call Timber the CFO – the Chief Fun Officer. When the guests come for a sled ride, he really likes to meet and greet them. He instinctively knows how to make folks happy.

Once a little girl who wasn't sure about getting in the sled basket for a ride started screaming. Timber pranced up to her and stole her mittens. He ran around with them. She ran after him laughing and squealing. By the time she got her gloves back, she was happy to ride. Atta boy!

Paws to consider:

Who helps you lighten up and smile?

Can you   play with kids?

lie on your back and let people rub your tummy?

see only the goodness in others?

How can you make someone else happy today?

Sister Poke

My name is Nugget and I'm a sled dog. I'm snow white. My sister Poke and I are Alaskan Huskies. But she looks more like the typical sled dog. In fact, they often use her for the poster child photos. She's really cute. She knows it too.

Otherwise, we are very much the same. We have identical running patterns. Teamed up, we ran side by side on the gangline. We prefer to run in the middle of the pack versus in the front or in the back. More than anything we really like to pull.

We both like treats but are skeptical when they come from strangers.

Another similarity is we like to bark, and we bark more than the whole rest of the team combined. I, however, will stop when told to do so. Poke has a lot to say and never stops barking. Consequently, she gets into trouble all the time for talking too much. Do you know anyone like that?

As siblings, we sometimes fight. I don't like when she sticks her nose in my food bowl. I also don't like when she steals my chew bone. Sometimes I wish she would just shut up.

Even though we are both over 13 years old, we still like to play together. We like to have fun, sniff human fingers and get our hind quarters scratched by them. Poke likes it a little more than me. She turns her behind to a perfect stranger and wiggles until they understand what she wants. She can have them scratch her all day.

Yet, all in all, I love my sister and she loves me.

Paws to consider:

How special is your family to you?

Do you   bark too much?
                wiggle your behind to strangers?
                steal your sister's bone?

When was the last time you licked up the remaining food from around your sister's mouth?

Hot Diggity Dog

My name is Nugget, and I'm a sled dog.

There are a lot of things people say about dogs. I think they need some clarification:

Work like a dog: Yeah. When you work like a sled dog, you are really working.

Tired as a dog: Yeah. When you have worked like a sled dog, feeling tired is satisfying.

You can't teach an old dog new tricks: Of course you can. Just give him a hot dog.

Hot diggity dog: Okay. I got this one figured out. When you get a hot dog, you get so excited that you dig a hole and bury it. Hot diggity dog!

Dog eat dog: I don't get this one. Unless you mean hot dogs.

Sick as a dog: This happens when you eat too many hot dogs. Particularly the old ones you buried.

Three-dog night: When you're out on the trail, and it's cold, you bring a dog into your tent. When it's really cold, you bring in two. And when it's super cold, three. Three dog night. I volunteer.

Lead a dog's life: Means a drab or boring life. Hmm. They must not be sled dogs.

Paws to consider:

What expressions define you?

Are you   a sly dog?

                a salty dog?

                a junkyard dog?

                a top dog?

How do you define others by the expressions you use?

San Juan Snow

My name is Nugget and I'm a sled dog. I love snow. Cold, crisp, clean. More than anything, I love to run on fresh snow.

In the summertime, we sometimes pull a four-wheeled cart, which is similar to a dog sled. We are athletes and need to stay in shape in the off-season, physically and mentally. Any pulling is better than none, yet I like it best when the sled is on a trail of packed,

soft snow. Some snow is soaking wet. Some are super flakey. I like the kind that falls in itsy bitsy little balls or grapple (a.k.a. corn snow). This stuff is slick and easy to pull a sled across. Fast snow. We get a lot of this in the San Juan Mountains, more than in the tundra of Alaska. I think we live in the best place for dog sledding in the world. (I'm the white dog in the picture.)

Normally, I sleep in my doghouse. Yet I like to sleep outside when the snow falls hard. I dig a small hole, curl up, and let a thick layer of snow cover me like a blanket. Perfect.

I often think that snow is God's gift of water, frozen and ready for another day. I can lap up snow with my tongue. Cool and refreshing. I might add that yellow snow is to be approached with caution. You know, dogs are required to sniff yellow snow. After all, one must determine from the smell if it comes from a friend or foe. Personally, I dislike the taste. However, Timber (a Siberian) rolls in smelly snow whenever he gets the chance.

Paws to consider:

What does snow mean to you?

Is it   a reason to play?

              a pain in the back to shovel?

              a blessing of water for the Springtime?

              a snowball fight waiting to happen?

What emotion happens inside when it snows?

Puppy Love

My name is Nugget and I'm a sled dog.

Everyone loves a puppy. They are small, whimsical, annoying, and well…CUTE. Our team just got six of them. (Someone was being playful again!)

They nip, they chew. They sleep, squirm, eat and grow. That's about it. That's all they do. They have little ears and little feet. Little tails and little mouths that go squeak, squeak, squeak.

Puppies are roly-poly bundles of love. They soothe the soul. Humans love holding sleeping puppies. They smile a different kind of smile when they have a puppy in their arms.

I really like the smell of puppy breath. It's kinda skunky, yet wet and wonderful. The smell of pure innocence, unconditional love, warmth and peace. There is nothing like being licked by a puppy that still has puppy breath.

When they are about nine months old, they will get harness-tested. You put a harness on them and see if they pull. If they do, they can join the team. If not, they become pets. To my knowledge, no husky has failed the harness test.

Paws to consider:

What are puppies to you?

> A source of unconditional love?
> A trusting source of peace?
> A ball of fur waiting to pee on you?
> A gift from God for a troubled soul?

Where will you find your source of puppy love this week?

Pooping Puppies

My name is Nugget and I'm a sled dog.

Sled dogs poop all the time. Like ALL THE TIME.

Most of us have learned to *GO* (out the backend) on the run. No problem. We just wiggle our buttocks and away it *goes*. Stepping on stools is not unusual. Of course, if there is a guest in the sled and a dog behind you kicks it in her face, then we might get yelled at. So that could be a problem. Just not necessarily my problem.

Now, not being able to drop a few is a real problem. The musher will bench us from running with the team if we haven't *gone* in a few days. Eating grass helps take care of constipation. Fiber!

There is a lot you can tell from the smell, consistency, and taste (coprophagia) of a dog's excrement: Illness, worry, fear, and even happiness. Yup. It's easy. Just take the scratch and sniff test. One of our Siberian Huskies named Timber likes to eat the stuff as much as a dog treat. So, the musher always warns the guests that he also likes to kiss strangers. Bagh.

Usually, I like to wait until I've stopped. Most preferably I *go* best near my doghouse, but never in my doghouse. My sister, Poke, always goes in the same spot. She is such a neatnik.

The musher likes to keep a clean dog yard. So, our poopies get scooped up at least once per day. Often, her husband does the scooping. This is a way he claims to show his love for his spouse.

Strange man. I thought human women liked flowers. Both are very aromatic, I guess.

Paws to consider:

What does scooping up poop mean to you?

Is it   a sign of affection?

a necessary evil?

a diagnostic tool?

a snack?

What happens in your mind when you have to *go*?

Nugget Food

My name is Nugget and I'm a sled dog.

In the end, we are all domestic animals. We do not hunt for our food. We wait to be fed.. Every day is a ritual of sleeping, eating, working, pissing and pooping. This is what we do. We wait all night for mealtime, which normally comes in the morning.

Early in the morning, my human will come out of the house to prepare the feeding.

Yes. Yes! YES!

The procedure is always the same. A quart of warm water is put in our feeding buckets. A scoop, one pound of kibble, is added. It is always the same kibble. This does not matter. It is food, and we love to eat it. If I do not eat it, it may be given to another dog. If I am loose, maybe I can steal a mouthful from another dog's bucket. This can go very wrong quickly. One morning I tried to steal a gulp of food from Mary's bucket. She got very angry. She about ripped my nose off.

Seriously. Food is serious business.

Paws to Consider:

Do you   live to eat or eat to live?

                    work to eat, or eat to work?

What is food to you?

A Sled Dog Retires

My name is Nugget and I'm a sled dog.

My sister Poke stopped pulling and the musher braked the team to a halt. Poke lifted her left paw. While not noticeably in pain, it was clear. No more pulling today. So she got to ride in the sled basket with her mother and an excited 2-year old human. After a week off, she was brought back to the team for another try at work. After a mile or so, same thing; stop, left paw up. Hmm. Two weeks later, same thing. "Well, Poke," says the musher. "I guess it's time for you to retire."

Poke and I are both 13 years old. She is proud of the fact that she is 37 minutes older than me. Yet, I do miss her on the trail. We always liked running together with the team. Now she gets to go inside and sleep next to the fireplace and eat biscuits. Lucky dog!

Poke and Nugget just before retiring.

Paws to consider:

Do you know when it's time to call it quits?

What is retirement to you?

> Is it a time to relax?
> Is it a time to start something new?
> Is it a time to reflect and be lazy?
> Is it a blessing?

How will you know that it is time to make a life-change?

P.S. It is time for me to retire from writing. My ghostwriter is no longer here to help. Goodbye!

Made in the USA
Monee, IL
18 December 2024

74570034R00125